ELMINA

Building on the past to create a better future

KIT Publishers

Colofon

KIT Publishers BV
Mauritskade 63
P.O. Box 95001
1090 HA Amsterdam
The Netherlands
E-mail: publishers@kit.nl
Website: www.kit.nl/publishers

© 2008 KIT Publishers BV, Amsterdam, The Netherlands/Government of Ghana represented by the National Authorizing Officer, Ministry of Finance & Economic Planning, Accra, Ghana

Editor-in-Chief: Ester van Steekelenburg, Urban Solutions, Rotterdam, The Netherlands

Production in Ghana: Judith Lekkerkerker, Urban Solutions, Rotterdam, The Netherlands

Interviewing: Stratcomm Africa, Accra, Ghana

Photography: Portraits and photos of completed projects by Nana Kofi Acquah, Accra, Ghana. All other photos by Urban Solutions.

Logistical Support: Anthony Annan-Prah, Nana Ekua Viala and Josephine Akoto-Bamfo

Design: Studio Wil Agaatsz BNO, Meppel, The Netherlands

Text editing: Stewart Brierley, The Netherlands

Printing: High Trade, Zwolle, The Netherlands

Implementing agencies: KEEA District Assembly, Elmina, Ghana & Urban Solutions, Rotterdam, the Netherlands
www.urban-solutions.nl

This book was financially supported by the European Commission.

Contents

Part I : The Elmina 2015 Strategy   6

Part II : Elmina Before-After   48

Part III: Elmina Portraits   100

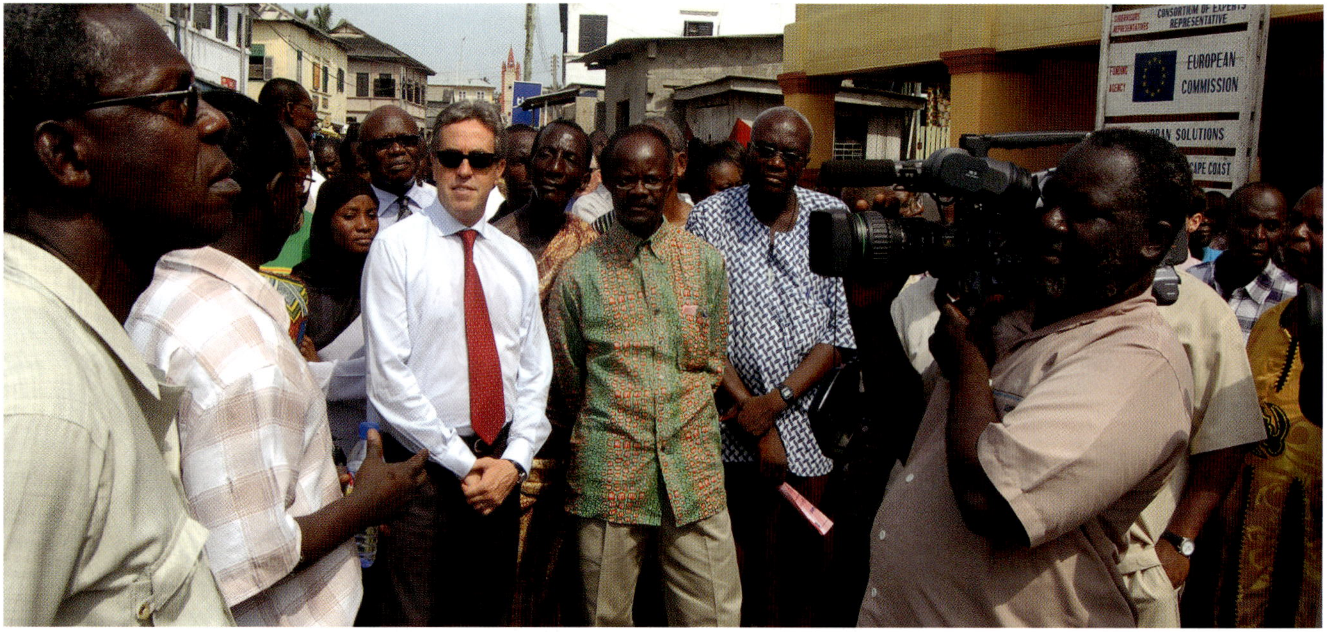
REPRESENTATIVES
CONSORTIUM OF EXPERTS REPRESENTATIVE
AGENCY
EUROPEAN COMMISSION
SOLUTIONS
CAPE COAST

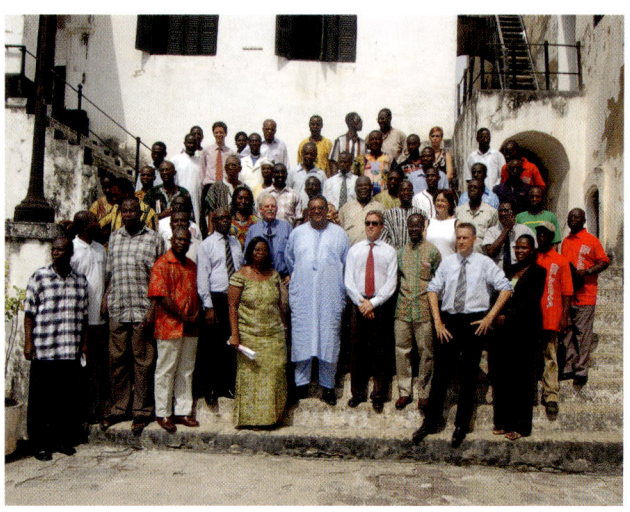

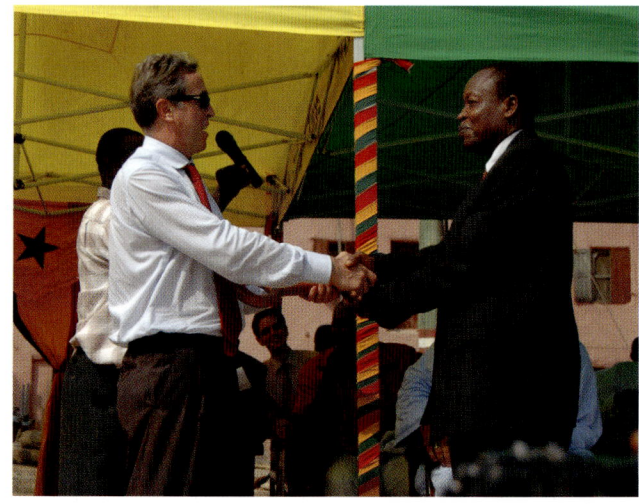

Foreword

This book on the Cultural Heritage and Local Economic Development project in Elmina aims at showcasing the results of a successful development cooperation project in Africa built on the economic use of cultural heritage.

Ghana celebrated its 50th anniversary of independence in 2007 but the history of Ghana is much older and Elmina is an important part of it. The castles and forts are not only a reminder of Ghana's past trade links with Europe and a legacy of its colonial past, they also represent a symbol of the slave trade and as such, form a beacon to the Diaspora of the descendants of West-African slaves. It was not easy to intervene in Elmina, a place so marked by its complex history, but the chosen innovative approach "building on the past to create a better future" was a very interesting one: acknowledging the past without ignoring the future and linking culture with economic development to improve the lives of the people of Elmina.

Recognising the importance of cultural heritage and its potential role for local economic development, in 2004 the European Commission agreed to support the project with almost 2 million Euros, funded through the 9th European Development Fund. The Elmina Cultural Heritage and Management Programme was established after extensive consultations with the local population and followed an integrated approach. While aiming at improving the living conditions of the people in Elmina, renovation of the sites and buildings of historical importance was also intended to increase the town's tourism potential and encourage tourists to visit Elmina, to stay longer and to spend more. This should generate more revenue, create jobs and therefore reduce the existing poverty of the residents. And this process has already started, since investors are showing interest and shops, hotels and even a clinic have already opened in some of the renovated historical houses.

However, renovating a monumental building or site is not enough. It should go hand in hand with building the capacity of the people. Monuments and historical sites should therefore not be considered as separate entities but as parts of the larger environment. Indeed, the European Commission would have missed an important objective without investing in the most precious resource of Elmina: its people. This is why within this project tourist guides, artisans and small scale entrepreneurs were trained in various fields, including in financial management.

Whilst reading the book you will no doubt compare the pictures taken three years ago with the impressive achievements of the project so far. You will also find lively testimonies from Elminian citizens to which the project brought tangible benefits and even changed their life. Indeed, we should not forget that the continuous success of the project is now in the hands of the people of Elmina.

I believe that this publication will provide visitors from all shores with a "taste" of Elmina and the desire to explore the beauty of this fascinating city.

F. C. Sebregondi

Filiberto Ceriani Sebregondi
Head of the European Commission Delegation in Ghana

Part I

The Elmina 2015 Strategy

This is Elmina

Elmina is one of Ghana's most famous historic towns. Its strategic location made it the heart of the West African gold trade in the 16th century. The name Elmina is derived from the Portuguese 'La Mina' meaning 'the Mine'. The impressive castle of St. George 'd Elmina dates back to 1482 and yet holds the status of Africa's oldest European building. When the Dutch took control of Elmina in 1637, they followed the Portuguese example of establishing their Gold Coast headquarters at the Castle and expanded it to its present form, making it one of the country's most prominent buildings.

Originally, the European commercial interest was in gold, pepper and ivory. By the end of the 17th century, a new type of trade was established on the Gold Coast: the trade in slaves for the plantations in the Americas. Elmina became an important distribution point for these slaves, which were brought from the hinterland. The Castle was turned into a temporary prison for many thousands of slaves. The slave trade, which lasted until the early 19th century, still marks a dark spot in the history of many European countries and Ghana.

All through the 15th to 19th centuries, Elmina thrived on a host of economic activities. In addition to the evident fishing and food production, a service industry also developed, offering transport, security and storage facilities. The population of Elmina grew from several hundred people at the arrival of the Portuguese in the 15th century to roughly 20,000 in the mid-19th century.

During their presence in Elmina, the Dutch left behind a firm footprint. They planned the so called 'new town' and built a number of defence works around it. Many European men, including high officials in the Dutch administration, married local women and the children from these marriages were regularly sent to the Netherlands for education. The Dutch also took advantage of the local Edina Bronya festival to iron out difficulties in their trade and relationship with the local authorities. Because of this Edina Bronya is also referred to as 'Dutch Christmas' and is still celebrated on the first Thursday of every New Year.

The Dutch abandoned the shameful slave trade in 1814 and in 1872 they sold their possessions on the Gold Coast to the British in exchange for the rights to Bengkulu on Sumatra, Indonesia. One year later, Elmina town was bombarded in a decisive response by the British to the refusal of the King of Elmina to accept the new rule. Accra became the centre of the British colonial administration and in the years that followed many people left Elmina.

Little development has taken place since those days. Elmina's population numbers 20,000, only a handful more than in the mid 19th century. The town that was once the capital of the Gold Coast returned to its roots with the fishing industry again supplying the main source of income.

Ironically, the absence of development on a significant scale is why the historic centre of the town is still largely intact; displaying a wealth of evidence of Elmina's illustrious past. Elmina Castle and Fort, the two UNESCO listed world heritage sites, featuring prominently in the itinerary of every visitor to Ghana, attract around 100,000 visitors a year.

Yet Elmina did not take advantage of the ever increasing stream of tourists. The surroundings of the castle were not attractive for tourists. Harassment by the youth ensured that only the persistent traveller ventured into town. The historic houses in the town showed their age and there was a sheer absence of places inviting tourists to spend their money. Even the beaches around town failed to entice the visitors because they were often scattered with litter, together with the clogged drains a constant reminder that the town's living standards were not good enough.

The Elmina Heritage Project

A collective European support to Ghana's renaissance
It was at the eve of the 300-year celebrations of diplomatic relations between Ghana and the Europeans that the Dutch, together with the local authorities in Elmina, decided to take up the challenge to work on a comprehensive development strategy for the historic town, taking their mutual cultural heritage as a starting point.

Involving the people
First step was to pro-actively approach the local population and ask them to prioritise their problems and suggest possible solutions. Meetings were held with just about anyone, varying from community and church leaders to hotel owners and school teachers. In 2002, a public Town Consultation was held, capturing an even a broader audience. The event even received royal attention: the Dutch crown prince Willem Alexander and princess Máxima were guests of honour during their first official state visit.

5 Priority sectors
The result of this participatory process was the *Elmina 2015 Strategy: Building on the Past to Create a Better Future*. The document went beyond restoring monuments. It formulated an integrated approach to dealing with the five priority sectors: waste, fishing, tourism, health and education. Outside the normal jurisdiction, a multi-disciplinary Task Force formulated some 80 projects to improve the local living standards and boost the local tourism industry. These projects were then marketed under the umbrella of the 2015 Strategy.

Five priority areas

1. Tourism & Local Economic Development
2. Fishing & Fishing harbour
3. Waste Management & Drainage
4. Education
5. Health

10 key projects
The European Commission was indeed quick to recognise the value of the built heritage and its potential role for local economic development. Together with the Dutch Culture Fund, they adopted 10 key projects from the 2015 strategy:

1. St. George's Castle: repair of entrance bridge and upper terraces
2. Fort St. Jago: renovation and landscaping
3. Tourist facilities in Elmina
4. Renovation of 15 historic houses
5. Construction of staircases to St. Josephs and Java Hill
6. Face lift of Nana Kobina Gyan Square
7. Renovation of 19th century chapel and community hall
8. Renovation of Dutch Cemetery and surroundings
9. Expansion of Catholic Museum
10. Renovation of 4 Asafo Posts

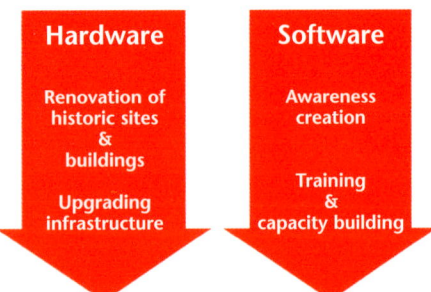

Hardware and software
It was not all about the hardware. In addition to the technical renovation works a substantial investment was made in the social infrastructure. A comprehensive training programme prepared the people of Elmina to take the maximum advantage of the improvements in their town. Would-be artisans, tour-guides and local entrepreneurs learned the tricks of the trade.

Local investment
For the people of Elmina the process was not without cost: a substantial investment was asked from the beneficiaries of the project, both in terms of time and money. Albeit hesitantly at first, the people of Elmina fully embraced the idea and this ensured local commitment and funds for future maintenance.

Spin-off effect
The Elmina Heritage Project had a tremendous impact on Elmina town that went well beyond the direct results of the 10 projects. The project has put Elmina firmly on the tourism map and higher on the political agenda; it also created a momentum for development and spearheaded a number of public and private investors coming to town to take advantage of the new opportunities.

Additional investments in infrastructure
The coastal highway has been upgraded, reducing travel time from Accra from four to three hours, basic services such as water, electricity, public transport and telephone coverage are being improved. The bridge over the lagoon has been renewed and perhaps most importantly: dredging of the Benya lagoon has commenced under the funding of Belgium.

Employment created locally
All contractors working on the renovation projects had to hire a maximum number of local staff to make sure that the projects worked as an employment-generating machine. More than 10 different contracting companies and consultants were hired and at the height of the project as many as 500 people were working on the different building sites throughout town.

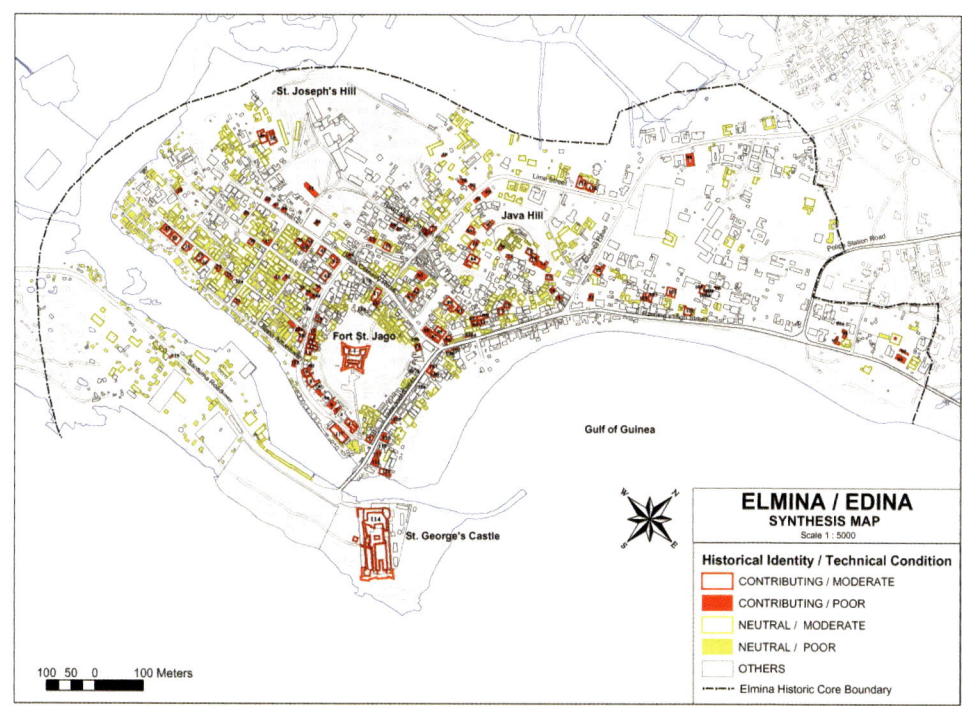

Keeping traditional skills for the future

The renovation works in town provided ample opportunities for Elminians to become qualified in the special restoration techniques of historic buildings. A selected number of workmen and artisans were coupled to the different renovation projects to learn the skills "on the job" and revive traditional building techniques.

Business coming to town

Local entrepreneurs were also quick to cash in on the increase in visitors. In recent months already four bar/restaurants have expanded their business, all reporting a significant increase in patronage from visitors and locals alike. In addition, other industries are discovering Elmina. Kakum Rural Bank has recently opened a branch in Elmina, the town now also has a very popular Internet café, and a Chinese/Ghanaian fish-processing plant has been constructed, providing employment to over 150 Elminians.

Making Elmina a better place

Environmental awareness has improved; people take more care of their surroundings. Slowly but surely, Elmina is becoming a cleaner and healthier place to live, work and play: *BUILDING ON THE PAST TO CREATE A BETTER FUTURE*

Nyimpa a ŏrofow dua pa no, wopia n`ekyir.

Give support to the one who is making good effort to climb.

Interview with
Sir Dr. Anthony Annan-Prah, Local Project Coordinator

Date: 3 October 2007

Sir Dr. Anthony Annan-Prah is a senior lecturer of Veterinary Sciences in Agriculture, Microbiology, Food Hygiene and Public Health at the University of Cape Coast. His family is from Elmina, He travelled to Europe for his studies but returned to serve his hometown. Because of his academic background and profound knowledge of Elmina's people and history, Dr. Annan-Prah became involved in the Elmina Heritage Project as the Project Coordinator. He is also active in the Catholic Church. In appreciation of his longstanding services to the community and the Catholic Church Sir Dr. Annan-Prah was knighted by the Pope with the Order of St. Gregory the Great in 2007 and invited to Brussels by European Commission President J.M. Barroso to be a witness of success of EU funded projects across the world.

Sowing the seeds

Around the year 2000, the Ghana Museums and Monuments Board (GMMB) planned to rehabilitate the St. George's Castle in Elmina. In connection with this, GMMB had contacts with officials from the Dutch Institute of Housing and Urban Development Studies (IHS, and later Urban Solutions), who gave a further suggestion that Elmina had no advantage financially from the mere visitation to the castle only if visitors did not stay in Elmina. They indicated that the castle should be linked to the town and, that the town and Castle must be developed together. We began to discuss *'What can we do to make Elmina vibrant and attractive to ourselves as residents and to foreigners as visitors'*. As such we began the process that formed the basis of the Elmina 2015 Strategy.

> 'In the assessment of the project we should consider that the impact is not only physical. It is also emotional and attitudinal'.
>
> 'When you restore private houses without asking a contribution, as it happened in nearby Cape Coast, the owners will not feel responsible for future maintenance of their properties.'

In the beginning of the process, people just thought out aloud, there was no structure. Therefore our task was to structure the problems. In order that it would not appear that the strategy emanated from an office and was dumped on the people, we wrote a preliminary report, which we called the Elmina Profile. This report captured our history, strengths, weaknesses, opportunities and threats. We held consultative meetings in the various constituencies of Elmina to think about the problems of the town and what we should do.

The people of Elmina met in a conference to validate the Elmina Profile and more importantly, to prioritise the problems in Elmina. The conference coincided with the visit of the Dutch Crown Prince Alexander and Princes Máxima and attracted many people and the press to Elmina.

Plenty of ideas but where to find the money

After the validation we started to write the Elmina 2015 Strategy. A Task Force was instituted by Urban Solutions, and the problems were categorised in five priority areas.
All the problems put together per category would form such big projects that they would require a great deal of capital, which is not easy to source. Therefore, these projects were broken down into Action Plans: what we can do within a

specific time frame and for what budget; what we can do ourselves and what needs external support. There were about 80 action plans. These were marketed and many people became interested, both foreign and local.

The greatest financial contribution came from the European Commission, about 1.5 million Euros. The EU ambassador was one of the guests of honour when the Crown Prince of the Netherlands visited. The EU fell in love with Elmina and the town's efforts in writing a strategic plan. The EU financial support resulted in the 10 projects to renovate the monuments and historic sites complemented by an elaborate awareness creation and training component.

Project planning, implementation and sustainability

We had set up Working Groups for the various projects. The Working Groups were very important in the development and implementation of the plans. The Working Group for the renovation of the Nana Kobina Gyan Square, for instance, changed the original plans to better suit the needs of the people. It indicated that the square needed to be used by the people and so planned gardens and trees had to make room for a functional square where large events could take place.

There was also a Working Group for the renovation of historic houses, made up by the owners of the properties. First of all, they played an essential role in the development of the architectural plans and now the group has been transformed in a Home Owners Association that manages the maintenance fund for the houses. So the Working Groups evolved over time to play a different role.

With regard to the sustenance of the rehabilitated historic houses, the contribution that was asked from the home owners towards the cost of rehabilitation was a very good initiative. First of all their contributions have been put into a maintenance fund. Furthermore, when you restore private houses without asking for a contribution as happened in Cape Coast, the owners will not feel responsible for the future maintenance.

Factors for succes

How far we have come has been influenced by a number of factors:

The intellectual idea aspect of having a development strategy that was really developed, owned, and promoted by the local people has been very important in the project. The impact of the project in the town has been profound. In the beginning there was a lot of scepticism with the people. Elmina had a research fatigue! There had been so many researches before but nothing ever happened. But now that they have understood the project, now that they see the results, they are supportive of the project and hope for a continuation of these efforts.

The implementation of projects such as this one should be done by someone who is neutral, as each town may be politically and traditionally polarised. You need someone, who will be the face of the project, who is diplomatic, in order to obtain the participation of all. It was therefore also good to have an external Project Management Unit (PMU) with international involvement and later, a Steering Committee of local stake-holders. This organisational structure was important to control the funds honestly and not give way to corruption. It also greatly enhanced the chances obtaining contributions from international donor organisations. Their involvement sometimes led to some frustration with Ghanaian counterparts, but had it not been for Urban Solutions and the keen interest of the then Chief Executive, Hon, Steven Nana Ato Arthur, there would not have been any funding in the first place!!

The scheme of implementation required an office in Accra while I was the Implementation Coordinator here in Elmina. My tasks were multiple: I had to look after the successful execution of the directives of the PMU, I had to be the neutral player and uniting force for all the people of Elmina, I had to think outside the box to do what the PMU had not thought of doing but which actions would enhance successful implementation and I had to translate the European mind into the

African setting. The task of project coordinator was not an easy one. It was hard work; I usually slept four hours a day!

The people had to be informed and attitudes reformed, consistently and persistently, by all the possible means. Radio is the main line of communication in Ghana. Every Tuesday I was on the local FM station telling people about Elmina's history and value and about the project, I have cassettes with about thousand hours of radio! We also went to the schools. Education is important for the young, for them to better value the assets of Elmina. We hope that they will help their parents to have a maintenance culture with regard to the assets that we have.

You have to understand that there were many people who were sceptical about the influence of tourists on our city; they felt that tourism would lead to things becoming more expensive, that it would impact local culture and may encourage prostitution, etc.
We quickly realised that expectation management was the most important aspect in order to avoid misunderstandings and conflicts. However, sometimes management also has to do some unusual things, otherwise there is only talk and nothing is done.

Is Elmina a better place now?
The 2015 Strategy in combination with the first implemented projects had a spin-off effect. An offshoot was the involvement of the city of Gouda in waste management. They provided waste collection vehicles, dustbins and they are now setting up a plastic processing plant in conjunction with the District Assembly. With the assistance of Gouda, the town has become significantly cleaner.

Belgians heard about the Elmina Strategy. A Belgian dredging company, Dredging International saw the prospects and approached its own government to fund the dredging of the harbour. This is now being executed.

Chinese investors have established a fish processing plant in Elmina. This was in fact a coincidence of events, the place for the plant became available when an accidental fire burnt down an illegal slum and then there was also the Elmina 2015 strategy to further convince the Chinese company to build the fish processing plant.
Many local businesses have sprung up in the renovated houses. I am told the number of visitations to the castle and town has increased, but I do not have the figures.

Elmina has become an example to other districts. We have become known, and other districts are beginning to want to learn how we did what we did. There is a spin-off effect. I was actually invited to Brussels by Mr. Barroso, president of the European Commission to be a witness to the success. People now visit the website of the project and send me e-mails for clarification and information even about things I have no knowledge of!

Finally, in the assessment of the project we should consider that the impact is not only physical. It is also emotional and attitudinal. This has been a very successful project in both ways.

Sasema rŏfŏw sŏr a ŏdze odupŏnye kwanifa.

A twig in the forest wishes to see the sky, it uses an oak as the supporter.

Interview with
Hon. Nana Ato Arthur, Regional Minister, Central Region

24 October 2007

> 'The Elmina 2015 Strategy is now our road map for the coming years and everybody who comes in should be within our road map'.
>
> 'Elmina was an old town going down, now it is a new town going up'.

Nana Ato Arthur - an engineer and planner by training - was Mayor of Elmina from 2001 to 2005. Prior to his appointment in Elmina he worked as a management consultant at the State Enterprise Commission in Accra, to then move on and rapidly climb the ranks of public administration. His student years brought him to China and Germany, where he broadened his perspective and even managed to pick up the language. His achievements in Elmina were duly rewarded as the President promoted him to the position of Minister of the Central Region in May 2006.

From problems to solutions

The idea for the entire project was already conceived before I was appointed in March 2001. However, because of the elections, nothing had yet been done. The very moment I stepped into office I said *'this is something that should be done'* and decided that we should provide whatever support was needed. We started by setting up a technical group and various committees to prepare the Elmina Profile, an analysis of the existing situation, discussing it every week. I was leading the District Assembly in 'owning' the project. Everywhere I went, I talked about the Elmina Cultural Heritage and Management Programme until the plan was complete and then we changed the name to the Elmina 2015 Strategy.

What has been very important is that we had commitment from the National Government to support the process we started in Elmina. In fact, Ghana's most senior Minister, Hon. J.H. Mensah, played a key role in the project. His family is from Elmina. In his position as a government leader he could address ambassadors and tell them about Elmina. He sent letters and invitations on our behalf. In the end, the European Union and the Dutch Embassy funded the implementation of various projects under the strategy. The planning process was funded by the Dutch government.

The commitment of local stakeholders was also very important for the success of the project. We were happy to have the commitment of the Chief and the Traditional Council; without their support we would not be as successful as we are now.

The new Elmina

The impact of the Strategy has been tremendous, in all five thematic areas. One of those areas was fishing and the fishing harbour, the harbour is now being dredged with funds from the Belgian Government. Tourism was chosen as one thematic area because Elmina has great tourism assets and the Castle and Fort are listed by World Heritage. In the field of tourism we wanted to develop lower-cost accommodation in addition to the high-class beach resorts and chose to renovate historic houses in the town in which home stays could open up. We also looked at those things that are typical of the local culture and we therefore decided to restore the Asafo Posts.

I approached the local hotels and told them 'our city is filthy, people who come to Elmina complain about it and don't stay. Why don't you support us in cleaning up the city, so that when business comes it will stay?' The hotels agreed and now support the cleaning of the city with an annual contribution. With regard to the thematic area of waste management, the involvement of the municipality of Gouda has been important. They have helped us a lot. They brought a garbage truck, litter bins and they are now starting a recycling plant. They also provided an ambulance, which contributed to our objectives in the thematic area of health. We built a doctor's bungalow in order to attract a doctor to come and live in Elmina. At that time, there was no doctor in Elmina! However, a doctor is living there now.

The Elmina 2015 Strategy is now our road map for the coming years and everybody who comes in should be within our road map. We are very happy with the support of the European Union, the Dutch Embassy, our twin cities Gouda and Macon (USA) and other investors; they really looked at the strategy to see how they could support Elmina.

As a result of the Strategy, the number of tourists visiting Elmina has definitely increased, I cannot give you the statistics but we observe more visitors venturing into town and spending money buying a bottle of water, something to eat, etc. However, with regard to the notion of tourism for the people of Elmina, I must say we have not achieved the target yet. It takes time to have the people of Elmina understand the potential of tourism, for the town and for themselves but that will come when they are able to benefit from tourism.

It is all about the people and the process

When we reflect on the process over the last years, there were many good things. The involvement of Dr. Anthony Annan-Prah as the local project implementer gave the project the local touch, which was really important. People realised that it was their own project; it was no longer a project owned by some white people coming to do something for the people of Elmina.

Furthermore, it was important that we had the support of a team of consultants, experts in urban planning, which really helped in the planning process and in the implementation of the various projects. What also greatly helped the project was a regular release of funds, which was controlled by an external project management unit. Although the District Assembly could be considered the client of the project, we needed to have confidence in an outside player to take care of the financial management. At times this was difficult; after all we were the crucial players in the project.

The process of developing the strategy with the involvement of the various stakeholders is something that will be replicated in other municipalities. You need to have a good road map, a solid and well thought-out plan. You then need to go through the implementation stages and you will slowly achieve your aim. This requires some patience but also strong will and leadership from the Assembly.

Also in the region, we are actively promoting the planning tool that was used in Elmina. I tell other municipalities that we need to look at Elmina and replicate the planning process. As a result, some districts in the region are already seriously working on it. The German Development Service supports several initiatives by providing staff to assist the local government in the planning process.

As for lessons learned, I could say that first of all you need the commitment of the people to ensure successful projects. Strong leadership and commitment are essential in such projects. Furthermore, in Elmina we were supported by consultants, Urban Solutions, which was really helpful. Sometimes, planning is a complex exercise and you need a team that really understands the issues.

In the meantime, the KEEA District Assembly needs to continue with the project. We still have work to do to achieve all the objectives of the 2015 Strategy. It is also my responsibility, as regional minister, to push the idea in order to source the funds to continue the implementation of the strategy.

I would like to conclude by quoting Senior Minister Hon. J.H. Mensah: *'Elmina was an old town going down, now it is a new town going up'*.

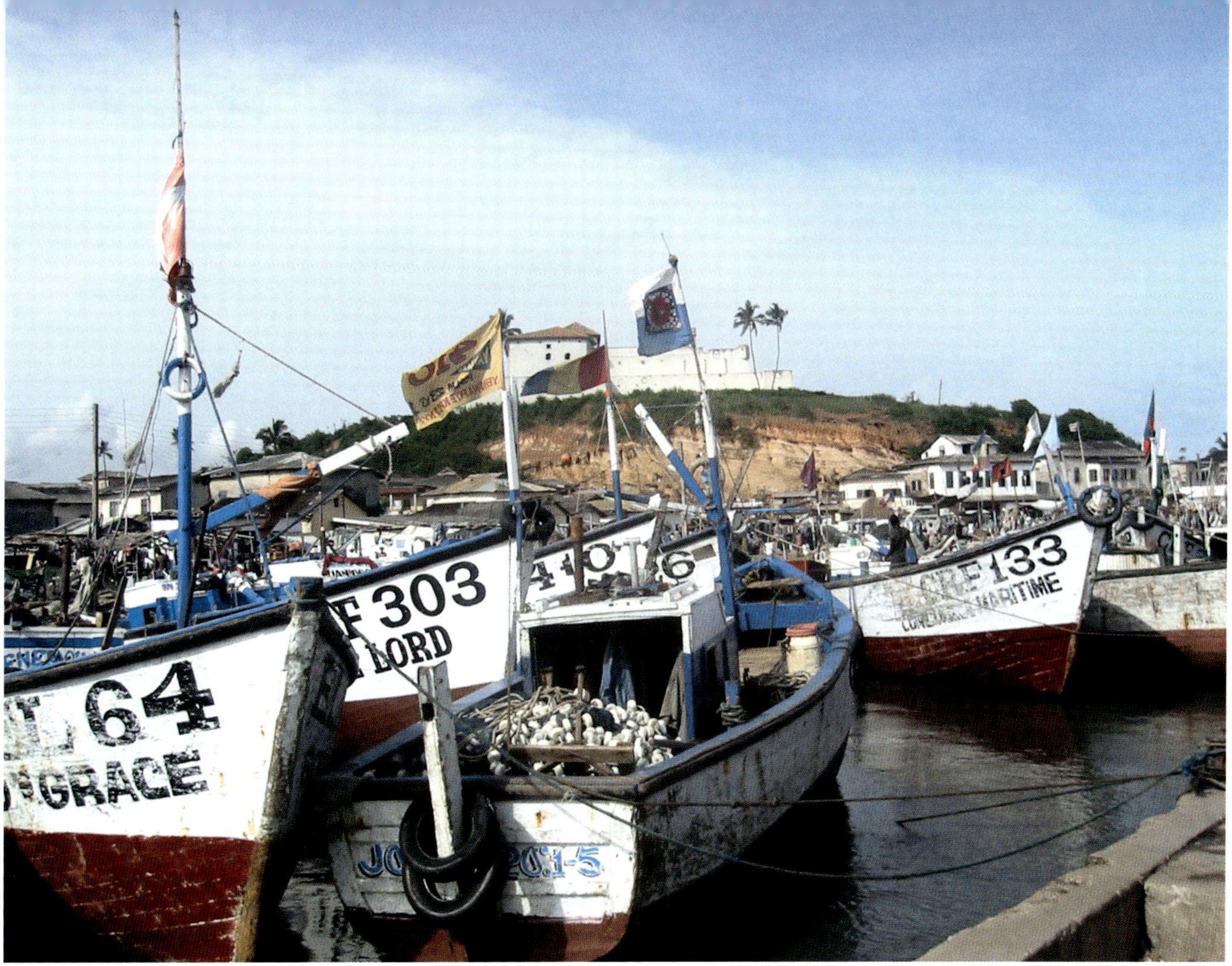
F 303
LORD
64
GRACE
133
MARITIME

SNAPPER COLD STORE
AND ICE
FACTORY
ELMINA

BELIEVERS

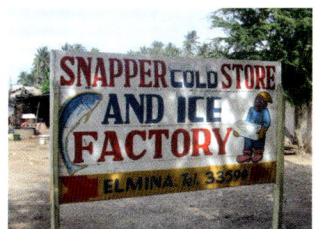

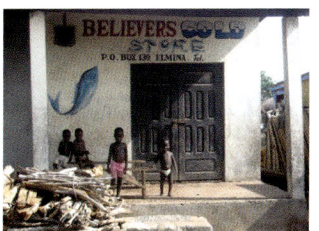

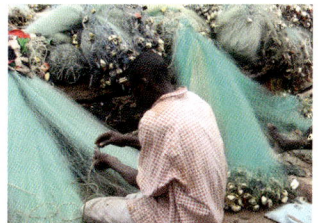

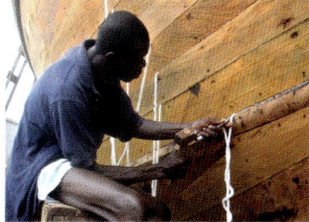

Womfa yafun pan nnhim aben.

We do not blow a trumpet with an empty stomach.

Interview with
Bridget Kyerematen-Darko, Managing Director of Aid to Artisans Ghana

19 October 2007

Mrs Bridget Kyerematen-Darko is the Executive Director of Aid to Artisans Ghana (ATAG), an organisation founded in 1988. ATAG is one of the key players in the Ghanaian handicraft industry, providing economic opportunities through craft development for the rural and urban poor. Headquartered in Accra's Trade Fair, ATAG has branch stores in several tourist destinations in the country. The selection is of top quality. They foster artistic traditions and inspire artisans to produce designs that appeal to both Ghanaian and Western customers.

Bridget, who holds a Postgraduate Diploma in Industrial Management and an MBA in Finance, has been with ATAG since 1993. She heads the management team and is responsible for the overall running. The Kyerematen family has their roots in Elmina, Bridget's maternal grandfather is from Elmina and the family house is still at Nana Kobina Gyan Square.

Recognising Elmina's potential

Elmina is a tourist area and Ghana is known for its culture and handicrafts. It was obvious that in Elmina there was a demand for cultural products, things for tourists to take home with them. Therefore, there was an opportunity for producers to obtain jobs and income. It was rather ridiculous however, that despite all this potential, tourism was not developed in Elmina. You would have thought that it would have arisen naturally. If there is a demand, people would normally fulfil it naturally.

> 'It was rather ridiculous that despite all this potential, tourism was not developed in Elmina.'

> 'It is the boats that are really a symbol of the culture of Elmina'.

> 'The trainees now do not just sit and wait for things to be done for them, they undertake action themselves to further develop the arts & craft production business in Elmina and that is a good thing.'

You would think that it does not need to be promoted.

For instance, a community could be traditionally weavers. Elmina is not traditionally a crafts area. Elminians are fishermen by nature; they are not weavers or wood carvers or whatever. It is the boats that are really a symbol of the culture of Elmina.

Starting from scratch

With regard to arts and crafts, there were some people active in Elmina but there were not enough skills to meet the demand. Actually, when we took up the project, we hoped to go in and find artisans already at work and help them with product development and marketing. However, there were almost no artisans in Elmina. We had to start with a number of them from scratch.

In the arts and crafts areas that we developed we tried to look at those products that tourists would like to buy and could also easily take home with them. We studied the local culture of Elmina - boats, fishing, history, trading - as a starting point for product development. We then combined this with traditional production methods - Kente weaving, tie & dye, bead making and wood carving - to create a distinctive Elmina product. The result was a number of marketable products with a local touch that could easily be produced by newcomers in the creative industry: small replicas of merchant houses, key-hangers and fridge magnets with boats, packaged bath salts etc.

It was a challenge for us to have the artisans appreciate the arts and see how they could respond to the culture and history of Elmina by the products that they make. All of them live in Elmina or were born there but we took them to the Castle several times to experience how tourists would see Elmina and to understand what products they could develop and sell.

Unfortunately, there were no skills available so we had to begin by developing the skills of the participants, which took time. This can be seen as one of the biggest bottlenecks in the project, it took us much longer than we would have hoped. Marketing and promotion skills were also lacking. It was difficult for them to understand the market they could have. For instance, they did not understand that making fridge magnets would be profitable. We can say that there was a big gap between the producer and the end-user, they tended to take instruction but they could not really understand why it should be done in a particular way.

Arts & Crafts for a living?

In total, 34 people have been trained over a period of 15 months. They have learned basic skills in one of the areas of arts and crafts and they have learned about product development. They are now able to make an income while they are further developing the skills of their craft.

With crafts it is obvious that people tend to appreciate a product more when they can see how it is made. That is why we launched the idea of an Arts & Crafts market, a central point where the artisans can produce and sell their products. Now that the Arts & Crafts market is finished, we are happy that its location outside the Castle is good, the emotional impact of a visit to the Castle does not have a positive effect on the purchasing behaviour of the tourists.

A very nice result of the training is that the participants in the training have organised themselves in an Arts & Crafts Association to deal with the local authorities and to be able to gain access to a credit facility. One of the artisans told me that they were thinking of taking a loan to fence off the Arts & Crafts Market to ensure safety during the night.

Local Psychology

An obstacle is that by definition projects are time bound. It took us three months to find the suitable participants and master craftsmen; it took us two months to identify a venue for the training to take place. This was not because of opposition but because of the disinterest of the people involved. For me, in development work we need to think carefully about the social aspects and the psychological impact. There are many issues that we take for granted when we start with these kinds of projects.

Last week I learned a nice lesson from the Queen Mother: Everybody who wants to hear 'yes yes' does great disturbance to himself. Everybody who is saying 'yes, yes', does not like the person they say 'yes, yes' to. The predecessor to the current Ashantehene once prepared palm wine and made sure it was overcooked so it became bitter. He invited all the chiefs and gave them the bitter palm wine. They all thanked him and said 'it is so nice, so nice'. He told them 'none of you like me, I know it's bad wine and all of you know it's bad wine too but not a single one of you could tell me the truth. You just wanted me to be happy and you were not honest with me.'

If you do not ask the right questions, you will never know what the answers should be. The right questions should not be asked just once or twice but maybe four times, to identify the real interests of people, to determine what they really want. For this aspect one should know more about psychology. This might help to avoid delays in the execution of development projects.

Lastly, I would like to say that it takes time for an entrepreneurial attitude to develop but I think the Elmina project can be seen as a big contribution to such developments. The trainees now do not just sit and wait for things to be done for them, they undertake action themselves to further develop the Arts & Crafts business in Elmina and that is a good thing.

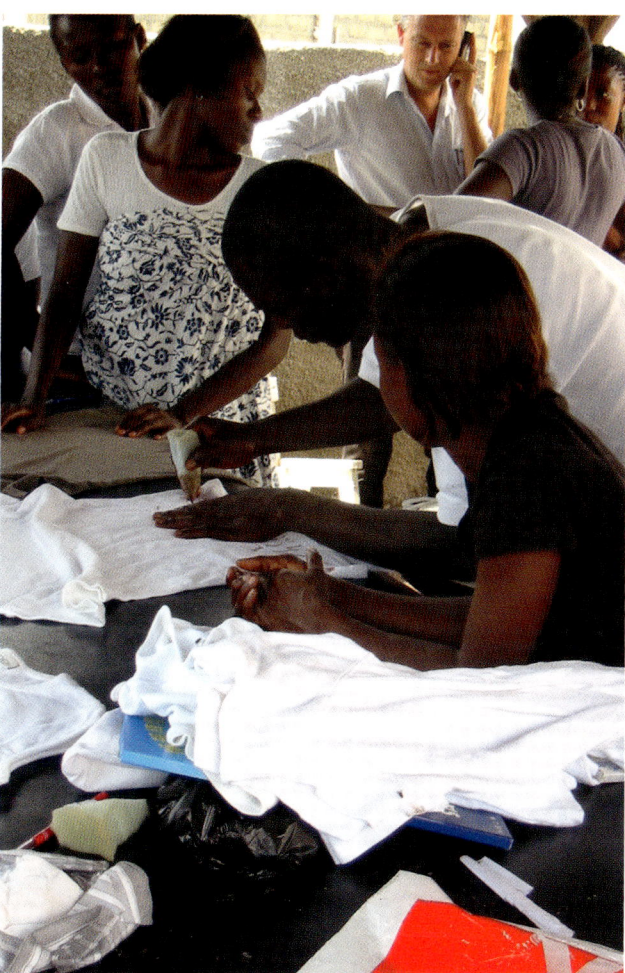

Kankahen apa Edinaman ho.

When the Dutch boat leaves Elmina will be on its own.

Interview with
Hon. George Frank Asmah, District Chief Executive

Date: 3 October 2007

> 'It was a resolution to shift emphasis from adhoc interventions to a more comprehensive method of solving the problems.
>
> 'If you do not have a road map you will get lost all the time.'

Elmina is the capital of a constituency that encompasses 4 traditional areas: Komenda, Edina Eguafo and Abrem (KEEA). George Frank Asmah is the District Chief Executive (DCE) – or mayor - of the KEEA District, which has a population of about 100,000. Prior to his appointment as DCE in 2005, he was news editor of the Ghanaian Times and the Vice President of the Ghana Journalists Association.

The facelift

The project is actually the baby of my predecessor (Hon. Steven Nana Ato Arthur). The Elmina 2015 Strategy is the road map for the development of the entire district. It was a resolution to shift emphasis from ad-hoc interventions to a more comprehensive method of solving the development problems of the historic town of Elmina for the benefit of the district in general. The basis of the 2015 strategy is formed by five thematic areas: education, tourism, fishing, waste management and healthcare.

The projects implemented so far have really transformed the township. Apart from the obvious works that had to be done to the monuments, there have been a number of projects that made improvements to the town: the face-lift of Nana Kobina Gyan Square being the most significant one. Also the private houses that have been renovated have had a tremendous impact for the people of Elmina.

Results!!

The main emphasis of the projects implemented under the strategy up to now has been on tourism promotion and development, but this has already had a ripple-effect on the other aspects of the strategy. The Dutch Municipality of Gouda supports us in establishing a plastics processing plant which will be operating by the end of next year and it will provide employment to an estimated 300 persons. The collection and processing of plastics will greatly improve the waste management in the entire district. Also the dredging of the lagoon will improve the sanitation situation.

A Chinese company came to establish a fish processing plant in Elmina, Kakum Rural Bank, Ghana's leading financial institution has just opened commissioned the building for its headquarters and since my arrival two new hotels have opened their doors. Of course the District Assembly is happy to see these improvements and investors coming to town. They bring employment, income and exposure.

A good example of where economic and environmental improvements come together is the Nana Kobina Gyan Square. It is being rented out for funerals, weddings, parties and meetings. It is a great source of revenue for the District Assembly. Cleanliness is off course vital for the attraction we desire to have and therefore we are happy to see that since the upgrading exercise those living around the square pay more attention to keep it clean.

Show me the road

If you do not have a road map you will get lost all the time. We have summarised our plans into such a road map: the 2015 Strategy. So at a glance you can easily conclude that this district wants to go this way. A strategy also enhances getting support externally. The district can realise a lot of aspects on its own, but certain aspects are very capital intensive. These aspects of course need intensive lobby for support and for that such a document is essential.

A man who had heard of the 2015 Strategy came to visit the KEEA District Assembly, we provided him with the complete document on a pen drive for him to take away. Two days later he came back, he had sent the strategy to friends in Israel who showed their interest in investing in Elmina. They will now come to investigate the opportunities themselves.

There is more to be done. Our plan is to develop the beachfront and the banks of the Benya Lagoon. Now that the lagoon is being dredged it is time to decongest the beachfront and transform it into a promenade with restaurants. People can even cruise on the lagoon, from the castle to Cape Coast and back.

In Africa there is information gap in many communities and districts. The information is there but it is incomplete and uncorrelated. Nevertheless in Elmina we have been able to dream and realise what we want. We are fortunate in this respect. Now it is time to look up to the future and realise the remaining goals of the strategy.

Ihu daamba sie a, ebŏ taku pŏw.

Take care of the pesewas and the cedis will take care of themselves.

Interview with
Hon. Jake Obetsebi-Lamptey, former Minister of Tourism

Date: 5 October 2007

> 'As the traditional source of income - the fishing sector - is declining, the development of sustainable tourism signifies a major improvement for a number of people and this will have a ripple effect on the entire community'
>
> 'I am a great believer in the five P's: Powerful Planning Prevents Pitiful Performance'

From 2002 to 2007 he was the Minister of Tourism and Modernisation of the Capital City. Jacob – his full name – is the second son of the late Emmanuel Obetsebi-Lamptey, a prominent lawyer and politician and his Dutch wife, Margaretha, or Auntie Margaret as she was best known. His parents met in London in the turbulent years after the Second World War. Jake and his brothers were schooled in the UK. In 1966 he returned to Ghana where he pursued an impressive career in media and advertising. In the 1980s he became director of Lintas, the leading marketing services company in the country ultimately employing over 300 people. True to the spirit of his father, he became involved in politics. He was one of the founding members of the New Patriotic Party (NPP). When Kufuor was elected President in 2000, Jake was his Chief of Staff and subsequently became Minister of Information.

Tourism as job creator

My first encounter with the Elmina project was in 2002, when the consultations with the different stakeholders in Elmina began. From the beginning I thought it was an excellent idea, and I still think it is an excellent idea.

Tourism is an industry in which Ghana has a tremendous competitive advantage; it is something which we have only recently started to develop. When we aim for growing the economy or restructure the economy, we tend to focus on the percentages and numbers of economic growth, but what it really is all about is the employment it creates. Tourism is very labour intensive and it creates jobs throughout the various classes, from the highly educated to the totally un-educated and is therefore an excellent development sector.

What we have seen in Elmina is that the traditional source of income - the fishing sector - was declining, and in that perspective the development of sustainable tourism signified a major improvement for a number of people. This has had a ripple effect on the entire community. The first tourists were harassed, but this has definitely decreased. With the different presentation of Elmina developed under the project, together with the improvement of the environment, tourists have begun to spend more time and more money in town. The people of Elmina are gradually learning that they can benefit from this as well. I strongly believe that in producing a more attractive place for tourism, we create a better place to live in.

Planning and performance

Every district has some document to show that there are talks about the development of the district, but almost invariably these almost the same as the documents of ten years ago, they are all written in this government language and different stakeholders were not involved. So there is no local ownership.

The great thing about the Elmina Strategy is that it started from a completely fresh page in the preparation of the development strategy. They really looked, with the involvement of the local people, at their district and what they could do to create wealth for the district, how they could develop it. When I was Minister of Information, we promoted development communications to create ownership of developed policies. A policy should not be something for politicians only; it should be for the stakeholders and agreed by all of us.

I am a great believer in the five P's: Powerful Planning Prevents Pitiful Performance. The idea of a town going through the full motions of preparing a development plan for that town, with measurable targets, has to be something that is replicated right across the country. The major lesson from the Elmina Project is that if you go through the whole planning process you will ultimately obtain very good results.

It was important that the management of the project was in the hands of an external organisation. People here tend to focus on problems, for an outsider it is often easier to find creative solutions. Especially when it comes to development of tourism products we need external people to help, because people here in Ghana often do not understand tourism and how places can be made more successful in attracting tourists. When we want to grow as an international tourist destination it is good to involve the target group.

Elmina is an example for others to follow

Tourists do not come here only to lie on the beaches, they want to learn about Africa, about the people and the culture and the history. We need to do something to preserve our history. I know it is a rather delicate issue, because of the emotions felt by people of African descent who visit the castles; needless to say that these places should not be regarded as ordinary tourist attractions but should be treated with respect. That is exactly what has been done in Elmina, they paid attention to sensitivities of all parties involved.

Elmina can be seen as a pilot. What I have been doing, is that I pointed out to different District Assemblies that they

should come and look at what Elmina did, and learn from it. Over 40 forts and castles in the country have been allowed to deteriorate; these are places full of history and culture both for Ghanaians, Europeans and Africans here and in the Diaspora. Elmina has shown that we can use our heritage to build a better future. Let us learn from that: It is time to put an end to the negative and begin the positive.

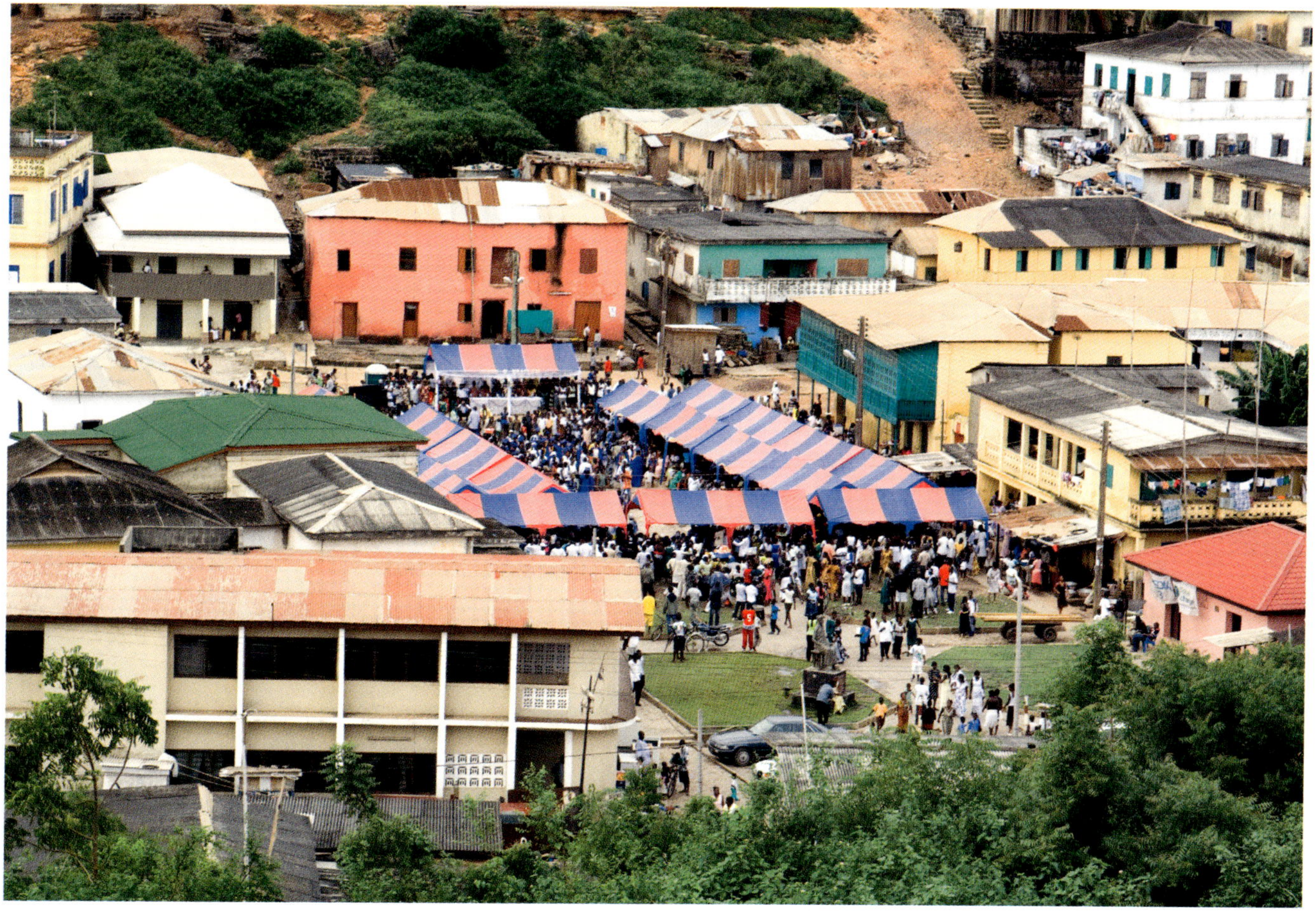

gramsdel j
REOPENING OF
gramsdel j

OPENING SOON
OCEAN VIEW INTERNET CAFÉ
TOMORROW'S INTERNET TODAY
LOCATION : ELIMINA.
OCEAN VIEW CAFE
OCEAN VIEW CAFE

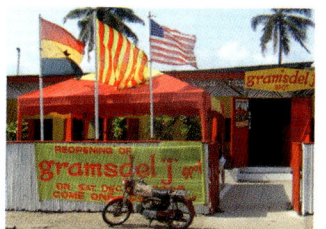

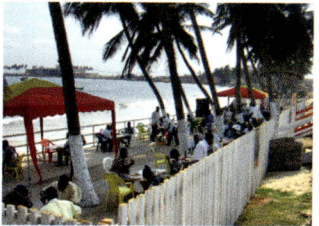

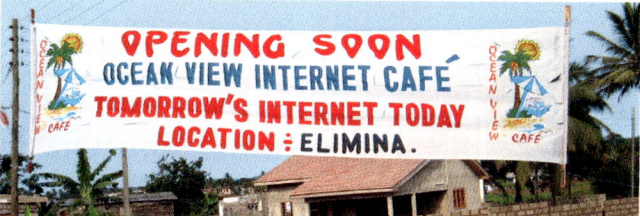

Hom nye asaase yi do nkyen, akokodurfo wo ahobrze mu.

You are the salt of the earth, courageous in modesty.

Lessons learned:

10 guiding principles for succesful project management

1   Do not look at Problems in Isolation

Use an integrated approach. There must be linkages between different economic sectors for any project to really develop and play a role in poverty reduction. For example, heritage conservation goes beyond buildings and monuments and the tourism industry cannot develop if the waste problem is not tackled simultaneously.

2   Combine Long-Term Strategy and Immediate Action

Define a long-term vision and meanwhile demonstrate a can-do mentality: show results in the short term with highly visible and tangible projects.

3   Manage Expectations

Be specific in what can be done in the foreseeable future, what the consequences are and how exactly people will benefit.

4   Get an Outsider's Perspective

Appoint an independent (outside) party to manage the preparation and implementation process. Sometimes a bold move is needed to get things moving. It also prevents conflicts of interest and promotes a solution-oriented process.

5   Think Globally, Act Locally

Be open to new ideas that have worked elsewhere but always relate them to the local context. As much as possible, use projects to generate employment locally.

6   Combine Hardware and Software

Do not ignore the social aspects and the psychological impact of a project. Let physical interventions go hand in hand with improvements in the socio-economic infrastructure.

7   Find an Engine for Growth

Find a unique selling point in a city and use it to source funding and generate interest from the media, politicians, investors, donor agencies, etc.

8   Find Commitment from Private Parties

Find the point where the driving forces of the public and private sector meet. Involve the private sector at an early stage to ensure their commitment to a jointly formulated roadmap.

9   Involve the Local Community

Invest in a participatory process. Involve the local community in both the plan formulation and decision making through a structured approach. Your return on investment is multiple: local ownership and political recognition,

10   No Free Ride

Make sure there is real demand and financial commitment for the projects that you plan. If people really want something they will find the money to pay for it. Invest now to establish a sound structure for maintenance in the future.

Part II

Elmina Before-After

PROJECT 1: Elmina Castle

Duration	:	9 months
Contractor	:	Akaidoo Enterprises Ltd
Consultants	:	Kwame Nkrumah University of Science and Technology, Kumasi (K,N,U,S,T)
Funding	:	€ 116,000, European Commission
Activities	:	- Repair works at the upper terraces and walls around the great court
		- Replacement of the bridges at the main entrance

World Heritage at risk

The UNESCO listed Elmina Castle was in danger of collapse. Built by the Portuguese in 1482 and later expanded by the Dutch it is a prominent reminder of the town's illustrious past. Being the first trading post built on the Gulf of Guinea, it holds the status of Africa's oldest European building. Despite over 100,000 visitors annually, maintenance was largely limited to obligatory repair works and odd painting jobs.

An examination in 2000 revealed that the structural condition of the Castle was in an alarming state and in fact, the upper terraces were unsafe. Critical cracks had developed in the walls and ceiling due to corrosion of the steel joints and chunks of concrete were falling off the walls. Because of imminent danger, the terraces were closed to the public in the 1990s.

Pulling up the bridge

A variety of repair works took place, the most important being the replacement of all steel beams and waterproofing the roof. In the rooms surrounding the great court, new doors and windows were fixed and the electricity was re-installed. Last but not least, the entire building was freshly painted, both on the inside and outside.

The concrete bridge that provides the only entrance for the public was about to collapse. Also, the sea wind had taken its toll. The reinforcement in the concrete beams that had replaced the original wooden structure and deck during an earlier renovation had started to rust and rot. The bridge had to be replaced completely. In addition, the drawbridge was replaced, modelled exactly after the original version. The Castle is now again safely accessible to visitors.

PROJECT 2: Fort St. Jago

Duration	:	8 months
Contractors	:	Memphis Construction Ltd, Kendricks Construction Ltd, De-bearacah Ltd.
Consultants	:	Ablin Consult, GW Consult, K.N.U.S.T.
Funding	:	€ 260,000, European Commission
Activities	:	- Internal repair to the Fort
		- Erosion protection and landscaping

Fort St. Jago: prominent building in a fantastic location

Fort St. Jago, originally named Fort Coenraadsburg, was the fortification from which the Dutch protected Elmina Castle. The four centuries old military fort was in a remarkable good technical state when the project started; it was partly renovated in 1995 with USAID funds. However, St. Jago Hill on which the fort stands was in poor condition: it was prone to regular landslides and indeed, in danger of collapsing due to erosion, fish smoking activities and illegal building. The houses surrounding the hill flooded regularly.

A future heritage hotel?

The Fort has served many purposes in its existence: police academy, hospital and prison. In the early seventies the fort was used as a low-budget hotel and once again the owner of the Fort, the Ghana Museum and Monuments Board, wants to take advantage of the fantastic location and put the fort into commercial use. Inspired by the concept of Paradores in Spain and former palaces in India that are operated as heritage hotels, a variety of possibilities is being explored: a conference centre, restaurant, hotel or inn.

To pave the way for interested investors, St. Jago hill has been terraced and landscaped and the road to the Fort and the drainage around the hill have been reconstructed. Furthermore, the doors, windows and floors have been upgraded and the roof on the well in the courtyard has been repaired.

PROJECT 3: Tourist facilities

Duration	:	12 months
Contractor	:	Allor & Sons Ltd
Consultants	:	GW Consult, SNV
Funding	:	€ 80,000, European Commission
Activities	:	- Establishment/ coaching of tourist office, signposts, tourism products
		- Construction of Arts & Crafts market

Elmina, Ghana's premier cultural tourism site

To establish Elmina as a must-go destination for cultural tourists, an attractive package of products has been put together that keeps visitors occupied in Elmina for several days. A number of initiatives have greatly improved the tourism infrastructure in Elmina:

Elmina Tourist Map

The Elmina Tourist Map was the first product of the Heritage Project. The map suggests a walking route that highlights the significant buildings and places of interest and offers background stories to understand the rich history of the town.

Signboards

Signboards have been posted along the walking route for easy reference.

Tourism Information Centre

A Tourism Information Centre at Nana Kobina Gyan Square is fully operational. The first of its kind in Ghana, it offers visitors a warm welcome, an introduction to the town, all the information they need on accommodation and bicycle and car rental. It also has a small souvenir shop selling postcards, T-shirts, maps and books.

Guided Tours and Organised Cruises

The Tourist Information Centre offers tailor-made Elmina packages for different target groups: a guided heritage walk, a visit to the fishing harbour and even boat trips on the Benya Lagoon and the open sea.

Arts & Crafts Market

Adjacent to the square an Arts & Crafts market has been constructed, here tourists can purchase high-quality souvenirs.

Website

The website www.encounterelmina.com was set up to give visitors from around the world easy access to practical information on Elmina.

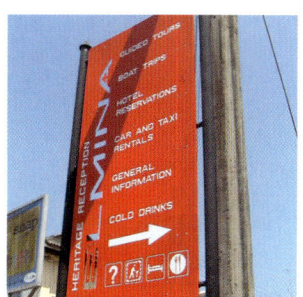

PROJECT 4a: Abraham House

Duration	:	9 months
Contractor	:	Llimpey Decon Ltd.
Consultants	:	Edward Nyarko/Qs-Pro, Tekton Consult
Funding	:	€ 21,000, European Commission
Activities	:	- Repair works to existing internal/external walls, floors and ceilings
		- Installation of doors/windows, electrical and plumbing works

Mr Abraham was a civil engineer by profession and supervised the construction of the house himself. He was a Nigerian national but married a Ghanaian and settled in Elmina. During the reign of Nana Di Ewu II (1936-1938), the house served as a Chief's palace. At the time, Abraham was a trader and hardly stayed at his home. It was when he was finally ready to settle that he took back his home. Originally, two 50 cm. tall porcelain statues of angels decorated the roof. The current owner still has one of them.

PROJECT 4b: Alfred Mensah House

Duration	:	9 months
Contractor	:	Llimpey Decon Ltd.
Consultants	:	Edward Nyarko/QS-PRO Consult, Tekton Consult
Funding	:	€ 41,000, European Commission
Activities	:	- Reconstruction of internal and external walls and facade
		- Restoration of roof, ceiling, floors, services installation and plumbing works

The Alfred Mensah House, dating back to the turn of the 19th century has a prime location at the junction of Nana Kobinah Gyan Square and Dutch Cemetery Street. It was in a very bad state and had indeed partially collapsed. Being a mud-brick house it had to be completely rebuilt from its first floor upwards. Experiments were done with different sizes of mud bricks in differing compositions, in order to determine the most suitable standard. In this way a model was developed that was also used in other mud-based properties, such as the Vroom and Kraal house.

After the renovation, the ground floor became the home of the Elmina Tourist Office. Due to its street corner location, the renovation had a tremendous impact on the look of the entire street. From the upper floors, the French windows offer a lovely view over the restyled square.

PROJECT 4c: Viala House 1

Duration	:	9 months
Contractor	:	Sammy Ray Construction Ltd,
Consultants	:	Edward Nyarko/QS-PRO Consult, Tony, Asare-Tekton Consult
Funding	:	€ 38,000, European Commission
Activities	:	- Reconstruction of dilapidated internal and external walls/facade
		- Restoration of roof, ceiling, floors, electrical installations, external works

The first Viala House was built in 1665 by Hubertus Varlet, a merchant from the Dutch town of Medemblik, for his family. When his son married Maria Bartels, daughter of the wealthy Bartels family, they built the second house. In 1853 Varlet died and two years later his son followed, leaving Maria a widow. Later, she married Albert Viala, a gold trader. The houses were named after the Viala family. After local tradition, Maria Bartels was buried in one of the rooms of her own house together with her son, Hermanus Albert Viala. Both gravestones are still intact. The location of the Viala houses was certainly among the most privileged for merchant houses in Elmina. To show their taste in the small colonial society of Elmina the Bartels family built in Palladian style, a typical European style, which has its roots in the Veneto region of Northern Italy.

PROJECT 4d: Viala House 2

Duration	:	9 months
Contractor	:	Sammy Ray Construction Ltd,
Consultants	:	Edward Nyarko/QS-PRO Consult, Tony Asare-Tekton Consult
Funding	:	€ 15,000 European Commission
Activities	:	- Repair works to walls, roofs, floors, ceiling and external works

The Viala House 2 was built by Albert Viala as an extension of the first one and shares the striking features and Palladian style façade. The façade, including the balconies, was reconstructed based on original photographs. Some additional structural repair work took place and new sanitary facilities were installed. During the renovation the unexpected ingress of rainwater caused one side wall to collapse. Traditional techniques were used to reconstruct the collapsed wall and to repair the existing walls.

PROJECT 4e: Conduah House

Duration	:	9 months
Contractor	:	Llimpey Decon Ltd.
Consultants	:	Edward Nyarko/QS-PRO Consult, Tony Asare-Tekton Consult
Funding	:	€ 23,000, European Commission
Activities	:	- Renovation and repair works to existing walls, roof, floors and ceiling
		- Electrical and plumbing, external works

The Conduah House, located adjacent to the fishing harbour was used as a warehouse for the storage of nets and other supplies. Now it houses a number of shops. The outbuilding suffered from concrete rot, a complicating factor for the renovation workers. The walls were repaired and floors re-plastered avoiding air pockets as much as was practicable.

PROJECT 4f: Chief Andoh House

Duration	:	9 months
Contractor	:	Llimpey Decon Ltd.
Consultants	:	Edward Nyarko/QS-PRO Consult, Tony Asare-Tekton Consult
Funding	:	€ 15,000, European Commission
Activities	:	- Renovation and repair works to existing walls, roof, floors and ceiling - Electrical and plumbing, external works

As the name suggests, this is the house of Chief Kweku Andoh, who became Chief of Elmina in 1873 after working for a European trading house in Cape Coast. During an expedition to Kumasi in 1895, he was assigned as personal advisor to Lieutenant General Sir Baden Powell who later founded the Scouting movement. The family still has a room with relics of Chief Andoh, including a palanquin. The house was modernised, the weak wooden floors were strengthened to provide stability and safety. After the renovation, the family managed to secure a 10-year tenancy agreement with the First National Savings & Loans bank.

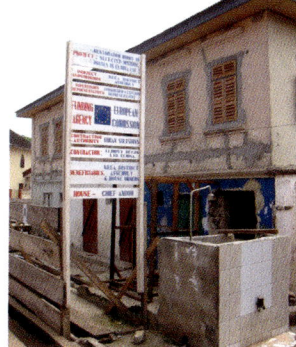

PROJECT 4g: Kraal House

Duration	:	9 months
Contractor	:	Llimpey Decon Ltd.
Consultants	:	Edward Nyarko/QS-PRO Consult, Tony Asare-Tekton Consult
Funding	:	€ 9,000, European Commission
Activities	:	Renovation and repair works

This house was originally a 'kraal' for cattle that grazed on pastures of what has now become Nana Kobina Gyan Square. Later, the house was used as a warehouse for imported gin. The house is the oldest existing mud structure in town. The walls were repaired and the house was re-roofed.

PROJECT 4h: Tiesman House

Duration	:	11 months
Contractor	:	Sambethy Investment Ltd
Consultants	:	Edward Nyarko/QS-PRO Consult, Tony Asare-Tekton Consult
Funding	:	€ 24,000, European Commission
Activities	:	Repair works to existing walls, roof, floors, ceiling and external works

The Tiesmah house is one of the most impressive properties along Liverpool Street. The unusually shaped house was constructed in 1934 by John Teschmacker. The Tiesma family (originally Teschmacker) are descendants of a Dutch merchant family. The house holds sacred ground as Emeritus Archbishop of Accra, His grace Dominic K. Andoh, preached from there. In recent years the ground floor has operated as a successful retail store selling household items. In addition to the structural repairs to the walls and floors, the kiosks obstructing the house have been removed and the shop front was revamped. The family is back in business.

PROJECT 4i: VanDijke House

Duration	:	6 months
Contractors	:	Sambethy Investment Ltd/Davies Wright Ltd
Consultants	:	GW Consult/QS-Pro Consult
Funding	:	€ 14,000, Dutch Culture Fund
Activities	:	- Repair works to existing walls, roof and ceiling,
		- Electrical and plumbing reconstruction of existing floors, external works

The Vandijke and Cornelius houses were built together, making it one of the largest houses in Elmina, prominently located along Buitenrust Lane ('Country-peace lane'). It is a rather strange name for an alley in one of the most densely populated town quarters in Elmina, however in the 18th century this was a quiet lane leading to the Government garden. The house was built in 1897 by Jacob Ruhle who designed the embankment of the Benya River in Elmina. The three-storey house has a central part, later extended with a wing enclosing a small courtyard. Part of the house was sold to Mr Van Dyke, a lawyer and also the author of the Edina State Constitution. Since the renovation, the elegant facade is occupied by a fashion and beauty boutique and the family rents out rooms to visitors.

PROJECT 4j: Vroom House

Duration	:	9 months
Contractor	:	Llimpey Decon Ltd.
Consultants	:	Edward Nyarko/QS-PRO Consult, Tony Asare-Tekton Consult
Funding	:	€ 17,000, European Commission
Activities	:	- Repair works to existing walls, roof, floors and ceiling
		- Electrical and plumbing, external works

The Vroom house was built in approximately 1900 by Hendrick Vroom, the son of Hendrick McCarthy Vroom, a mulatto commander of the Dutch resident army in Elmina. It has a prominent location overlooking Nana Kobina Gyan Square. The renovation works were rather elaborate. The foundation of the walls was weakened by the continuous ingress of rainwater from the roof of the neighbours. The wall was re-built and a gutter was inserted to the neighbour's house, to prevent further deterioration of the foundations.

PROJECT 4k: Jacob Essifilie House

Duration	:	9 months
Contractor	:	Llimpey Decon Ltd.
Consultants	:	Edward Nyarko/QS-PRO Consult, Tony Asare-Tekton Consult
Funding	:	€ 18,000, European Commission
Activities	:	- Repair works to existing walls, roof, floors and ceiling
		- Electrical and plumbing, external works

The innocent bypasser would not have noted the Jacob Essifilie house as anything special. However, since the renovation unveiled the original wrought iron support structure, it is one of the eye catching properties along Cemetery Street. The ground floor is occupied by a wholesaler of bottled drinks, while the upper floors house a Crafts & Coffee shop. The balcony offers a relaxing escape from the street's hustle and bustle.

PROJECT 4I: Plange House

Duration	:	11 months
Contractor	:	Sambethy Investment Ltd
Consultants	:	Edward Nyarko/QS-PRO Consult, Tony Asare-Tekton Consult
Funding	:	€ 25,000, European Commission
Activities	:	- Repair works to existing walls, roof, floors and ceiling
		- Electrical and plumbing, external works

Located at the beginning of Liverpool Street, Plange house stands out from the adjacent properties. William Plange was born in 1882 and died in 1964. He was a product buyer and merchant but also a statesman and one of the founding fathers of the Elmina Development Association (Edina Mpontu Kuw) and the Elmina Society (Edina Korye Kuw).

The ground floor of the house incorporates a sizeable courtyard. The chemical seller, who occupied the ground floor, has made place for a bicycle rental shop

PROJECT 4m: Bartels House

Duration	:	9 months
Contractor	:	Llimpey Decon Ltd.
Consultants	:	Edward Nyarko/QS-PRO Consult, Tony Asare-Tekton Consult
Funding	:	€ 26,000, European Commission
Activities	:	- Repair works to existing walls, roof, floors and ceiling - Electrical and plumbing, external works

Carl Ludwig Bartels, an officer in the Dutch army, was governor from 1789-1804. He married a lady from Elmina called Maria Cleriq and in 1786 built a substantial house for his wife and family in the old town, close to the river. The Bartels family is still one of the most prominent families in the country. This property served as Elmina's post office for many years. It is now used as a movie theatre and a shop selling bottled drinks.

PROJECT 4n: Ephson Aku House

Duration	:	9 months
Contractor	:	Sammy Ray Construction Ltd,
Consultants	:	Edward Nyarko/QS-PRO Consult, Tony Asare-Tekton Consult
Funding	:	€ 21,000, European Commission
Activities	:	- Repair works to existing walls, roof, floors and ceiling
		- Electrical and plumbing, external works

The Ephson Aku house is one of the most remarkable buildings along Liverpool Street. The stained glass windows have a unique floral pattern and were painstakingly restored. The upper floors were renovated with a keen eye on the architectural details while the ground floor was transformed into a retail outlet.

PROJECT 4o: Kweku Essuman House

Duration	:	11 months
Contractor	:	Sambethy Investment Ltd
Consultants	:	Edward Nyarko/QS-PRO Consult, Tony Asare-Tekton Consult
Funding	:	€ 24,000, European Commission
Activities	:	- Repair works to existing walls, roof, floors and ceiling
		- Electrical and plumbing, external works

This house was built by Nana Kweku Essun, a prosperous licensed surveyor from Elmina. It was once used as the Chief's Palace and it later served as a traditional bridal house. The founder of the famous St. Ceilia Singing Band in the Catholic Church, Choirmaster R.B. Eshun, once lived in this house. The house overlooks the Benya lagoon and fishing harbour. The family is yet to decide how best to capitalise on the facelift. A fish restaurant on the top floor is one of the possibilities.

PROJECT 5: Java Hill

Duration	:	6 months
Contractor	:	Marcobi Enterprise Ltd
Consultants	:	KEEA District Assembly
Funding	:	€ 10,000, Dutch Culture Fund
Activities	:	- Construction of staircases
		- Clearance of refuse dump

Java Hill is one of the three hills in Elmina. Originally, it was called Cotton Hill after the failed attempts to start cotton plantations during the 19th century. More successful was the recruitment exercise the government set up in the 1830s to enlist African soldiers for service in the Netherlands East Indies (Indonesia). The hill was named 'Java Hill' by the many retired soldiers who settled there after returning from their military service. They lived well from their pensions and built their properties accordingly.

In recent years the paths leading up to the hill were used as refuse dumps. The key elements of the Heritage Project were a number of infrastructural improvements, including the removal of the refuse and construction of staircases leading up to Java hill and the neighbouring St.Joseph's and St. Jago hill.

PROJECT 6: Nana Kobina Gyan Square

Duration :	8 months
Contractor :	Sammy Ray Construction Ltd
Consultants :	GW Consult, QS-Pro Consult Ltd
Funding :	€ 81,000, Dutch Culture Fund
Activities :	- Refurbishing Nana Kobina Gyan Square
	- Replacement of staircase on St. Joseph's hill

A square without identity

Located between the Methodist Church complex and the Dutch cemetery, a muddy stretch of land was the town's main public place. Ignored for many years, the square was slowly but surely being encroached upon. It served as a bus station, funeral venue and parking place.

Now once again the place to be

To retain and utilise the open space to its full potential, the project has landscaped the area and transformed it into a true public plaza where residents and tourists alike can come to relax, have a drink or enjoy a performance. The square is also the location of choice for the newly opened Tourism Information Centre and – in the near future – Elmina's first ATM machine. The square has been renamed Nana Kobina Gyan Square after Elmina's most famous Chief who was expelled from his country under English occupation. A statue to his memory now stands proudly in the middle of the square as a monument to the bravery of the Elmina people.

PROJECT 7: Nana Etsiapa Chapel

Duration	:	8 months
Contractor	:	Davies Wright Ltd
Consultants	:	GW Consult, QS Pro Consult Ltd
Funding	:	€ 47,000, Dutch Culture Fund
Activities	:	- Reconstruction of the roof
		- Improvement of sanitary facilities

The chapel without the roof

The Methodist Church complex located in the middle of town comprises three buildings: an old Dutch chapel, a school building and a church. The original Dutch chapel lost its roof in 1999 during a tropical storm; the building has since been without function. The adjacent pre-school was in a very bad state.

Community pulse is beating again

The local Methodist community restored the church in the 1990s. The Heritage Project followed suit and renovated the former chapel and pre-school. The roof of the chapel was completely reconstructed. The pre-school also received a new roof, all windows and doors were replaced, walls were freshly painted and the sanitary facilities were upgraded.

Nana Etsiapa Hall is now once again the thriving heart of the local community and is being used for meetings, exhibitions and cultural or sports events; the pre-school has been expanded with a children's library.

PROJECT 8: Dutch cemetery

Duration	:	3 months
Contractor	:	Davies Wright Ltd
Consultants	:	QS-Pro Consult
Funding	:	€ 21,000, Dutch Culture Fund
Activities	:	- Repair works to the graves, walls and entrance gate of the cemetery
		- Landscaping of the surroundings

An Elmina landmark

The Dutch cemetery, which dates back to 1806, is located in the centre of town and is surrounded by centuryold big silk trees that function as important landmarks in Elmina. Originally constructed to be the final resting place of the Dutch settlers and their descendants, it became the place for burying important Elminians, among which are the former king of Elmina, Nana Kobina Gyan and Dr R.P. Baffour, Ghana's Ambassador to the UK for many years and founding vice-chancellor of Kwame Nkrumah University of Science and Technology at Kumasi. The original gate of wrought iron carries the old Dutch saying: 'Zoete moeder, neemt uw kinderen weder' meaning 'Almighty mother, take back your children'.

History unveiled

Over the years, the tombs and vaults were overgrown by tree-roots, the gate and wall were damaged and one of the silk trees collapsed. The project newly landscaped the cemetery grounds, cleaned the graves, installed plaques with information on the buried and built a new gate. Also, the surrounding area benefited since a once muddy path leading up to St. Joseph's Hill has been replaced by a proper staircase.

PROJECT 9: Catholic museum

Duration	:	4 months
Contractor	:	Sammy Ray Construction Ltd
Consultants	:	GW Consult, QS Pro
Funding	:	€ 22,500, Dutch Culture Fund
Activities	:	- Renovation of existing museum and provision of furniture
		- Extension of ground floor

A hidden gem
In a cramped room at St. Joseph's Hill, the classification museum was hardly appropriate for the collection of historic Catholic relics. The building was hidden and the random visitor would find the door locked. The unique collection was simply gathering dust.

Properly polished for the public
The Heritage Project has, in cooperation with the Catholic Diocese of Cape Coast, transformed a former Catholic Boys School into a new home for the impressive collection: beautiful relics, such as a golden drinking cup from the 17th century, diaries from missionaries in the 19th century, the clothing of all the bishops of Ghana's Central region and an impressive set of the Stations of the Cross in Elmina by an African (or Black) Jesus. The museum also tells the story of the historic significance of Elmina in the world. It is part of the heritage walk and includes a friendly reception for visitors.

PROJECT 10: Asafo Post

Duration	:	4 months
Contractors	:	BCG Contract Works, Witlas Enterprises Ltd.
Consultants	:	KEEA District Assembly
Funding	:	€ 35,000, Royal Netherlands Embassy
Activities	:	- Rehabilitation of Asafopost 1, 2, 4, 5
		- Reparation and repainting of statues

European heritage and local tradition
During the 18th century, the wards in which Elmina was divided constituted themselves as army units: the Asafo companies. They adopted flags and other European-inspired regalia that they gradually modified for local use. As well as defending the town against local enemies, they developed an intense local rivalry, which was acted out during local festivals and other ceremonial occasions. Their active fighting role has long gone but the Asafo companies remain key in the ritual life of Elmina. During festivals, durbars and funerals they present themselves in their uniforms carrying flags, drums, brass instruments and firing guns.

Being restored to their full splendour
The Asafo companies have shrines in which relics are kept. The four most spectacular shrines – numbers 1, 2, 4 and 5 were decorated with statues set in an almost surreal combination of themes drawn from the Bible, the sea and the military. Over the years the shrines had deteriorated to a very poor state, even the once vivid colours could no longer hide their state. Now the Asafo Posts have been completely renovated and are open to visitors, offering them a unique experience of viewing these shrines and hidden treasures from the inside.

Abesifo (No. 5) Asafo Post
The Abesifo company was the so-called navy company, hence the ship. The ground floor is ornamented with its supi, the Queen Mother of the company and two women carrying sacred objects on their heads. The crab symbolises the skilfulness of the Asafo members.

Ankobeafo (No.1) Asafo Post
This Asafo Post features a key as an emblem, which is a vital element in the rites for the titular god of Elmina, Benya. On top of the building is a replica of the dome of the Benya shrine, the god of the Benya lagoon.

Akyemfo (No.2) Asafo post

The proverb on the shrine of the number 2 company is said to refer to the shed under which the Portuguese captain, Don Diego d'Azambuja, agreed with the Elmina King, Kwamena Ansa, to purchase the plot for Elmina Castle. The eagle represents the company's courage. This shrine is accompanied by the company symbols: the two airplanes.

Wombir fo (No. 4) Asafo post

The shrine of the number 4 company, Wombir, is the most spectacular in town. The statues of Adam and Eve symbolise that this was the first Asafo company in Elmina. The animals at the shrine refer to the hunting activities of the company and of course there is a scene that portrays the sea and fishing: the mermaids on the first floor balcony. The shrine is crowned by a crocodile, which symbolises the fearlessness of the company.

Part III

Elmina Portraits

1 Touring the new Elmina

Name : Glantist Essandoh
Occupation : Tour Guide
Age : 32 years
Children : Two

The struggle for greener pastures

I started life as a video photographer. Business in Elmina was not very good. I had to travel to Accra for a job. My wife and my children hardly saw me because I was away most of the time. Each time I left home it was very painful.

I heard about the programme for training tour guides organised by the heritage project. I decided to enrol. I thought to myself, maybe life will smile at me again. We were divided into three groups and I trained as a marine tour guide. The training was good. I learnt how to handle tourists as well as how to guide them on a cruise on the sea and lakes.

Cruising the sea and lagoon

I am now a professional marine tour guide. I take tourists on boat rides. I make sure they have their life jackets on before we set off. Elmina has some exciting and unusually attractive sites on the sea and the lagoon. I show them the site where a school of fish will be playfully jumping in and out of the sea. The tourists are often very happy to see this spectacle. They take a lot of pictures. I also take them to a bird sanctuary near the lagoon, where migrating birds converge. The highlight of the tour is 'dwarf island' where legend says dwarves used to live.

Happy at home

I do not have to travel out of Elmina to earn a living. I see my family all the time and my income is regular to take care of my family. I begin each day with a lot of hope because the project has helped to attract more tourists into Elmina town and they spend more time and money here. Before the project, the youth of the town rushed to the tourists and frightened them away. Tourists would normally go from their hotels to the Elmina Castle and go back to their countries because the town did not look very nice. Now our Elmina is beautiful and clean. The project is changing our lives economically and things look good.

> Working as a tour guide is now my profession and I enjoy it and it earns income for my family. I see my wife and child every day and I do not have to travel too far to earn a living.

2 Carpet on the table?

Name   : Madam Anna Carson VanDyke
Occupation : Rtd Secretary
Age   : 65 years
Children : Three

A house filled with memories from the past

Vandyke house is our ancestral home, built in 1897 by a Dutch businessman who settled in Elmina. This house is full of history and we have captured its historical past with memorabilia, pictures and paintings. One of the pictures on the wall is that of the first Van Dyke to settle here in Elmina. These pictures and the decorative china pieces displayed are relics from the past to tell visitors our story. The living room here is the place that engages one's attention in my house. This centre table is covered with what is called a "floor carpet" and this is what my ancestors used to cover their tables during their stay at Elmina, so I have kept it that way.

The historical background of the house led to its selection for restoration under the Home Owners Scheme of the heritage project. I paid only ten per cent of the cost of rehabilitation and the rest was spread over a number of years. It was a very good bargain indeed. Before then, this house was virtually uninhabitable so it stood deserted. I only came once in a long while to ensure that there were no squatters in residence.

History is alive again

The heritage project restored my roof, reinforced the weak areas with concrete and applied fresh paint to the building. I see such a total transformation. I feel like I am dreaming. We have converted the whole top floor of this house into rooms for rental to visitors and tourists. We are planning to start a restaurant in the compound to serve guests, the public and tourists, to generate more income. Apart from the money we are earning from the room rentals, the house has beautified our street.

The whole family is very excited and happy about the restoration project and this is drawing them back home. They come with their friends from Accra and other parts of the country to show off the house. We even received a Dutch visitor, also named Van Dijke, who brought documents showing that we are distant relatives.

> This centre table is covered with what is called a "floor carpet" and this is what my ancestors used to cover their tables during their stay at Elmina, so I have kept it that way.

3 Golden choice

Name   : Wilhelmina Mensah
Occupation : Bar Operator
Age   : 56 years
Children   : Two

Place to be

My drinking bar is known as Golden Better Choice Spot because I believe it is the best relaxation joint with golden services in Elmina. My spot is located at the Nana Kobina Gyan square. Until the renovation of the square through the heritage project, the muddy and unkempt nature of the place kept customers away. After the renovation project, the square now looks nicer and more pleasant and this has attracted a lot of customers to my spot.

My spot is patronised by tourists and visitors who enjoy my services and my choice of music. My sales have increased; business is good even beyond the fishing season. The educational programmes given to the townsfolk on how to handle tourists under the heritage project have helped to draw tourists into the town.

Renewed joy and beauty

We are all very happy with events in Elmina. As a Queen Mother, I can now afford to buy proper regalia to adorn myself appropriately for the outdoor ceremony for Chiefs and Queens during festivals. Since the general facelift programme for Elmina took off, the aesthetic beauty of the town has become very evident and it is attracting a lot of people to the town. The exercise itself has generated jobs for the youth of the town. Visitors are surprised at the transformation and they even ask who has done this.

What has been done so far has contributed immensely to putting the town in shape. I look forward to seeing the craft shop fully operational because that will not only bring more tourists into town but also generate more income. There could be more performances by cultural groups to provide indigenous entertainment to tourists.

Tourism has a great income generating potential and already tourists are feeling free and happy and are willing to spend more.... Patronage of the spot has gone up and my sales have increased.

4 Face lifting

Name   : Nana Poku
Occupation : Engineer
Age   : 37 years

Elmina impressions

I began my tour of Elmina with the 'wow factor' here in the Castle. I will go deeper into town to see other interesting areas. From what I see today, I must admit it is better than before and the general feeling is good.

I left Ghana for the first time eleven years ago. I visited Elmina in 1996 and I tell you, the town needed a good facelift. I visited the Castle last time I came to Elmina in the company of a group of people, and the tour guide did a very bad job talking about the history of the Castle. I was disappointed at the sight of the town and the way the story about the castle was told. The story is better told this time. It is important that the facts are not confused, because it takes a lot of travelling to come this far.

Our heritage …getting it right

The Castle and the little I have seen of the town on my way here is not bad. The town looks tidier now. It would be even better if the wooden shops were cleared and the original use of the old buildings restored. An idea is to have people role play life in those days. I tell you if these forts and castles were in Europe or the United States, they would have been restored completely with the appropriate furnishings used by the colonial masters at the time. There would be people dressed in costumes such as soldiers, slaves, etc.

In the UK, where I have come from, there are a lot more people interested in Africa. As a tourist and a Ghanaian, I see these buildings as part of our heritage; all black people spread over the globe in a way take their roots from here. We should not wait for other people to invest money to restore our cultural heritage for us.

> I visited the Castle last time I came to Elmina in the company of a group of people, and the tour guide did a very bad job talking about the history of the Castle. The story is better told this time.

5 Uphill battle

Name : John Ebow Assifuah
Occupation : Retired Railway Worker
Age : 67 years

Java Hill...what's in a name?

When the Europeans settled here they came up the hill to erect their cannons because the location gave them a long and wide view of Elmina town and over the ocean to sight approaching enemy vessels. The cannons are still positioned here and they are now objects we sit on.

Why the hill is called Java Hill is an interesting story. In the 19th century, soldiers from the Gold Coast were recruited to serve in the Royal Dutch Indies Army. I believe some 1,000 recruits were sent from here to Indonesia. The people there must have been surprised by the appearance of blacks in the Dutch army. They gave them the name Belanda Hitams (Black Dutchmen). Some of these soldiers stayed in the East after their service but most of them came back. They lived together on Cotton Hill, whose name soon changed to Java Hill. These soldiers also brought with them the batik technique to make the wax-prints that are now so popular.

Conquering the mountain

Those of us who live up the hill used to just climb the rough ground daily to reach our homes. Probably, we were born mountaineers so we have been climbing this hill ever since we were born – men, women and children. When we slip and fall, we pick ourselves up and continue our upward or downward journey. For over 60 years, I have been climbing this hill. Living on a hill is not an easy thing. My people become tired so they throw garbage on the side of the hill instead of going down to dispose of it properly. Over time, a heap of refuse developed here and it was indeed a health hazard and an eyesore.

Java Hill was fortunate to be part of the heritage project and we now have a well constructed staircase to go up and down the hill with much ease. Our refuse dump has been cleared and the area is now very tidy. It has been of great help to the whole community. We are happy these developments are at last coming to us up here at Java Hill.

> Those of us who live up the hill used to just climb the rough ground daily to reach our homes....now we have a well constructed staircase to go up and down the hill with much ease.

6 Building a future

Name : Winnifred Essien Bilson & Randolph Kuntu Blankson
School : Edinaman Secondary School
Age : 16 & 18 years

Changing scenes
We first heard about the tourism project at a durbar during the school holidays. Our friends and the pastor at church also talked about the project. The information we had was that our town square, the Nana Gyan Square, would get a face-lift and some of the old houses in town would also be renovated.

Winnifred:
The square used to be a market with all the associated chaos. It then became a lorry park, another bustling activity and now we have the full glory of the Nana Gyan Square, a peaceful park that we use only for major public and social events. It is very beautiful now. We recently had a book market and a trade fair there. People from various regions attended the fair. I like it as it is now.

The town is also very clean now. As a child, I could not move freely around town because there was refuse all over the place. Now there are nurses in town educating people about hygiene and cleanliness. My mother is a caterer and she sells cooked food to the public. Flies used to worry her and business was not so good but now her work area is very neat and this has increased her business. I am learning hard to be a journalist when I grow up so I can continue the sanitation campaign. It is very important.

My mother is a caterer. Flies used to worry her and business was not too good but now her work area is very neat and this has increased her business. She can now take good care of me and my siblings because she can increase her sales and profits.

7 Stones from Zion

Name   : Solomon Donkor
Occupation : African textile & art works producer
Age   : 27 years

Preparing for tourists

This shop was given to my brother and I by ATAG as part of the heritage project. The condition was that we had to participate in a year long training programme. The idea was to help the youth in the town to acquire some skills to begin the craft market here.

You should have seen the poor state of this piece of land before the project came in. It was very unpleasant. The land was a dumping ground for discarded construction materials such as wood and stones. There was stagnant water and wild grass all over the place. Now we have a craft market here to support tourism. The environment here has greatly improved; the atmosphere is good and welcoming.

> We are very optimistic about the success of the market because we have done our research and we know the tourists will like our products.

My childhood dream coming true

Making art pieces is my life. From childhood I had the desire for art and my mother encouraged me. I went to art school and studied picture making and graphic design. I understand art and I appreciate the opportunity to train others in art work production.

My brother and I have been selling here since January 2007. The name of our shop is 'Zion Stone'. We sell miniature drum pieces, fishing vessels, calabash pieces decorated with African symbols, African jewellery, jewellery boxes and several other different pieces. Sales were slow initially but it has picked up over the months.

Tourists are now trickling into the shop. They are getting to know about the existence of the craft market. I am confident that one day this market will be bustling with activity.

The income generating potential is very high, so we are not ready to give up on the shop here. We are very optimistic about the success of the market because we have done our research and we know the tourists will like our products. When business is good we sell about 10 GHC worth of products now. We are targeting tourists and footballers who will be coming to town for the African Cup of Nations (AFCON) 2008 tournament and I expect sales to be massive.

8　Cleaning campaign

Name : James Gmakame
Occupation : District Environmental Health Officer
Age : 48 years
Children : Five

Making Elmina clean

At a big meeting held sometime in 2001, tourism was identified as one of the five critical development pillars in the KEEA District. In that meeting tourism was directly linked to improvement in sanitation. Elmina is one of the important tourism locations in Ghana but due to poor sanitary conditions tourists were unwilling to stay overnight here when they visited. The people of Elmina themselves raised this concern and made an exercise to clean up the town a major priority.

Winning the sanitation war

To arrest the situation, we secured refuse containers and placed them at vantage points in town. These are regularly collected and emptied at a designated disposal point. The Assembly also acquired a 16-acre refuse disposal site with support from our partners and our Netherlands sister city Gouda. They also assisted us by providing 500 portable litter bins.

We embarked on an education exercise to raise sanitation awareness in the communities. Sanitation inspectors have also been going around the communities to ensure that people abide by the law or otherwise face sanctions. We recently fined a company for creating unsanitary conditions and the court ruled in our favour. This has served as a good lesson to the Elmina community. Sanitary recalcitrants are fined between 10 and 50 GHC.

The people of Elmina are happy to see that dredging of the Benya lagoon has begun. Several other activities are taking place to ensure that we win the sanitation war. We had difficulty financing our sanitation and tourism plans but the heritage project has enabled us to move forward.

Since we took charge of the sanitary concerns we have seen a major difference. There has been a major improvement in the health of the people. I can confirm that the incidence of conditions associated with unsanitary conditions has gone down. These include malaria, cholera, typhoid and dysentery.

Our tourists are assured of a clean environment. Already some tourists are beginning to spend nights in our town and this is a good sign that we are winning the sanitation war. This is just the beginning.

> Already some tourists are beginning to spend nights in our town and this is a good sign that we are winning the sanitation war. This is just the beginning.

9 Catch of the day

Name   : Nana Solomon
Occupation : Chief Fisherman
Age   : 50 years
Children   : Three

Fishing - our livelihood

The fishing industry here is as old as the town. It is the main livelihood of my people. I can say that about 65 per cent of the local community are engaged in fishing. We also have migrant fishermen from other parts of the country who have settled here for this trade. As Chief Fisherman of Elmina, I speak for my people. We are a political force here. Our job is a man's job because it is difficult. There are so many hardships and mysteries on the high seas. We therefore protect and support each other. We are always out there wrestling with the sea for sustenance. We sometimes win with a bumper catch and we sometimes lose the fight and come home empty handed.

> We are always out there wrestling with the sea for sustenance. We sometimes win with a bumper catch and we sometimes lose the fight and come home empty handed.

Elmina – land of our birth and heritage

Elmina is our home. We love the place and want to contribute in any way to support its growth and development. That is why it first saddened me that the project was about the monuments and not about the fishing harbour. We saw some houses being restored and other things being done. The Asafo post project was very important for our fishing community, it is now completed.

I must say the town now looks good. Sanitation is improving so I can say that the heritage project has positively impacted the town. The project attracts tourists and other people. It generates more interest for our industry and opens up Elmina for more jobs. Perhaps this will offer alternative means of livelihood here; some of my men may opt for them.

Now the harbour is being dredged by people from Belgium. This is a good thing because it was difficult for the vessels to get into the lagoon. The fish processing plant is also new, a Chinese-Ghanaian joint venture and it makes the local fishing industry more professional. My people feel proud it has come to Elmina. Projects such as this come and go but we will always be here. This place will always remain our home.

10 Story telling

Name : Francis Kofi Arthur
Occupation : Leader, Blessed Family Cultural Troupe
Age : 45 years
Children : Seven

The power of culture

Elmina is a community rich in history and culture. As a teacher I realised our rich culture could be tapped through drama. This motivated the establishment of the Blessed Family Cultural Troupe, four years ago. We now have a membership of 50 people between the ages of 20 and 45 years. We practice every week. Our performances are developed around ancient stories and cultural ceremonies. We keep these stories alive. The District Assembly and the Elmina Tourist Board have invited us on several occasions to perform at public functions, festivals and for tourists. We have a drama series currently running on the local radio station to educate the community about civic responsibilities.

When the heritage project took off in Elmina, we saw an opportunity to be part of the project to showcase Elmina to tourists and use drama to make our people a part of the whole effort to raise the image of Elmina to attract tourists for the benefit of our community.

Festival revival

The project organised a number of cultural evenings at the Nana Kobina Gyan Square. One was a drama contest for the different cultural troupes in Elmina. Although we did not come first, it was very exciting to be part of it. Hundreds of people came out to watch and a famous radio DJ was one of the judges. Another event was a rock concert, it was like in the old days of high-life music, everybody was out there dancing and enjoying themselves.

I must say that the heritage project has been very useful to Elmina. Now we have the restored Nana Kobina Gyan Square where we hold our performances. We do not charge for our performances now but we hope to do so soon to raise funds to take care of our needs and to provide an allowance for troupe members. We are proud to share our rich culture with visitors and tourists and ultimately generate funds for ourselves.

> Our performances are developed around ancient stories and cultural ceremonies. We keep these stories alive.

11 Home coming

Name : Mabel & Rabbi Kohain Halevi
Occupation : Owner, Mabel's Table Hotel & Restaurant
Age : 63 years
Children : Two

Finding our roots

A few years ago, a group of us in the Diaspora in the UK, took the decision to relocate to Africa. We are now the repatriated community in Elmina. I have no regrets. For me, this is my real home coming after years of sojourning. I settled here and started a restaurant by the seaside. From here you have a wonderful view of the coastline and the Castle and there is a refreshing sea breeze. We serve local dishes but also things that the tourists like such as battered fish & chips and pizza. Since the restaurant business was good we also started to rent out rooms. There was a need for medium priced accommodation in town in addition to the three-star beach resorts. Most of our guests are Africans from the Diaspora who come here to find their roots.

> The Castle stands as a witness to a dark chapter in our history. The story is not pretty but it must be told in order that people never forget what happened here. Therefore it is important that the heritage is preserved.

Apart from running this hospitality business I am also interested in black history and tourism and I belong to the Panafest foundation. Panafest is a Pan-African historical cultural festival organised every two years, bringing thousands of people to Cape Coast and Elmina. The theme for 2007 is 'Re-uniting the African Family'.

Keeping heritage alive

From time to time I take tourists to historical sites such as the Elmina Castle. The Castle stands as a witness to a dark chapter in our history. The story is not pretty but it must be told in order that people never forget what happened here. Therefore it is important that the heritage is preserved.

Having been involved in tourism for several years now, I appreciate the value of putting Elmina in shape to maximise its attraction to tourists. The heritage project is therefore a good thing. I heard about the project from some of my clients who visited my restaurant. Then, as I passed through town, I saw the Elmina 2015 Strategy sign boards and some restoration work going on. Then I knew something was really happening. I must say the project has enhanced the aesthetic beauty of the town. We are happy that something good is now coming out of something that was once so bad.

12 Fishing for the future

Name   : Zuewen Zhang
Occupation : Manager, Elmina Fish Processing Plant
Age   : 34 years
Children   : One

Investment potential

We started working in Elmina in 2005 but I came ahead of our team in 2000 to begin the process of establishing our industry here. We settled here because from our assessment, the volume of fresh fish landed in Elmina by the local fishermen could adequately meet the raw material needs of our business. This informed our decision to locate our business here. Though the indications we had from our background checks and research showed that the fishing industry is good, we were worried about the general environmental situation.

I feel excited about the growth of the fishing industry here and my company will offer training to fishermen to help them increase their catch.

Things are looking up

The dredging of the lagoon has helped to revitalise the fishing industry. Before then the lagoon had silted to the extent that some of the fishermen moved out of the area because the landing space was inadequate to accommodate all of them. There are now over 500 boats in the lagoon and the industry is thriving. I am excited about the new turn of events. The future of the fishing industry here looks bright.

I feel upbeat about growth in the industry here and my company will be working with the regional and district authorities to offer training to the fishermen to help them improve their skills to enable them to increase their catch. I have employed 27 local people. We are also regulating our fish purchases to ensure that women in the fish smoking industry have fish for their business.

The heritage project has greatly improved the sanitation and health conditions in Elmina. I was here and I can attest to the radical transformation that has taken place. The face of Elmina is changing positively. The poor sanitation situation is giving way to a clean environment. I can see houses being renovated and a lot of fresh paint all over the place. The town is looking bright now and visitors feel safe, health wise, venturing into town.

13 Entrepreneurial spirit

Name   : Pee Nana Gyekye Quainoo
Occupation : Manager, Shell Station
Age   : 48 years
Children   : Two

Elmina illusion

For over 15 years I watched with sadness as tourists came in bus loads, spend a couple of hours at the castle, refuel their coaches and left for other destinations. Each time, I told myself, there goes a good opportunity to make money for Elmina. The town with all its rich history and interesting sites did not benefit economically from the tourism industry in Ghana.

The environment was in poor condition and most of the old buildings were falling apart. Elmina could not be described as a welcoming haven for tourists. Additionally, my people did not know how to treat tourists. The people were friendly but sometimes their friendliness was intimidating because they pestered tourists for money. They think the white man has more money.

> I watched with sadness as tourists came in bus loads to spend a couple of hours at the castle, refuel their coaches and leave for other destinations.

Building business

I operate a Shell station. It used to be just a fuel station with a small convenience store but in recent years I have expanded my business. I now have a drinking spot and an Internet café. To target travellers I also advertise the clean toilet facilities. This station is well located on the busy road from Cape Coast to Takoradi. The stretch from Winneba to here used to be very bad with lots of potholes but in the past two years a new road has been built. It now takes just three hours to travel from Accra to Elmina.

I have noticed that the facelift project has put Elmina in the spotlight as a tourist destination. I admit the project has contributed a great deal to preparing the town to attract visitors. This was a first deliberate official effort to get them to stay on longer here.

I think it is important to have a strong travel and tour arrangement with linkages outside the country to market the restored houses and their history, our festivals, indigenous food and other activities that will encourage tourists to stay and spend money in Elmina. The project gave us a base for the take off of the tourism industry; it is now up to the people of Elmina to take it one step further.

14 Gold coasters

Name : Nana Tanoh
Occupation : Traditional leader
Age : 64 years
Children : Five

Our heritage our home

The links between the Europeans and the Elminians are centuries old. In 1481, the Portuguese started trading with the chiefs of Elmina. The Europeans left their footprints here. Of course we have the fort and castle to remind us of the past. But when you look more carefully you find evidence of our links with the Europeans everywhere in town. The Elmina flag for example has the same colours as the Dutch flag. We also find many Dutch names in Elmina: Vandijke, Bartels, Vroom, Nagtglas and Tiesmah.

I have lived in Elmina all my life. As one of the chiefs of Elmina, I have always held discussions with other chiefs in the traditional area about ways of bringing income generating activities to Elmina to enhance the wellbeing of the community. Our only problem was how to create diverse job opportunities. Fishing is the only major industry in the community. I was part of a series of meetings held to plan the execution of the project. It became obvious that there was a need for a face-lift of the town to enable us to achieve our objective of making tourism an income generating project.

The Europeans left their footprints here, when you look carefully you find evidence of our links with the Europeans everywhere in town.

The turn around - perfect timing

This project came at the time when things were really bad around town. Some of the old homes that were built by the Europeans had collapsed and had been deserted by the owners for lack of funds to rehabilitate them. There were sanitation problems to deal with and residents did not care much about keeping the environment clean.

This situation has completely changed. People visit Elmina and cannot help but admire the new look of the town. This has impacted on the increase in the number of tourists and visitors to our town. We need a lot of such projects. It has made a lot of difference to the economic wellbeing of our people. Is the project going to be continued? The people keep asking.

15 Trading places

Name   : Father Peter Adokor Enchill
Occupation : Parish Priest, St Joseph's Minor Basilica
Age   : 53 years

Roots rediscovered

Elmina is where Christianity in Ghana started. In the early 16th century the Portuguese built a Franciscan church on what is now St Jago's Hill and dedicated it to St George, it was the first Christian church building in sub-Saharan Africa. The Europeans also brought education; at the order of the Governor of the Elmina instruction in reading, writing and religious education took place within the Castle walls. In fact, the best known Castle school on the Gold Coast was the one operated by the Dutch at Elmina.

Elmina is a community immensely rich in history. This is an asset which can be harnessed to turn around the fortunes of the community. The heritage project could not have come at a better time to facilitate the restoration of Elmina to its old glory.

Dusting relics of the past

The museum at St. Joseph's benefited from the heritage project. The weak woodwork structure of the museum was changed and concrete applied to strengthen it. The museum itself holds important historical pieces such as models of the forts and castles built in Elmina by the Dutch explorers and traders; busts of bishops and priests who headed parishes; old mass vessels; vestments for priests and bishops; gold vessels and monstrances used for benediction. These relics are of immense interest to our visitors.

Since the restoration work on the museum began, visits by tourists have increased significantly; sometimes we have 5 group visits a week. This is very encouraging. Because of this, the Parish Priest has employed a full time tour guide to take care of the visitors.

When I visit my people they talk about the changes with a lot of pride. The change can also be felt among our fishermen who are taking advantage of the dredging exercise to improve their businesses. This project is a God send and I hope it will continue to enable Elmina to reach its full potential.

> When I visit my people they talk about the changes with a lot of pride.

16 Awakening

Name : Christopher Ewusi
Occupation : Manager, Elmina Tourist Office
Age : 32 years
Children : One

Elmina…sleeping beauty

The heritage project is goal specific with a focus on tourism. The project aims at essentially adding value to existing tourist attractions in Elmina as well as preparing the community effectively to welcome visitors. Before all this, tourism was dormant here in Elmina. Ironically, tourism can best be described as Elmina's pot of gold. The people were sleeping away income and tourism was far from organised.

> I must say that for the people here, the project is a life saver. Today tourism is clearly defined and structured in Elmina. Visitor inflow is peaking from virtually nothing to about 10-20 a day.

She's slowly waking up

I am the manager of the Tourist Office. It is the first of its kind in the whole country. We moved into our new premises at Nana Kobina Gyan Square last year. We assist visitors to find transport and accommodation. We have also organised walking tours around the heritage trail, a lagoon cruise and even a cruise that takes you out on a fishing canoe at sea. People have to wear life vests as it can get quite rough out there. We try to tailor the products to the different target groups: Europeans, Afro-Americans and domestic tourists. We receive very positive feed-back especially concerning the level of detail of the information provided.

We obtain additional income from selling postcards, Tee shirts, maps and bicycle rental. Most revenue however, is generated from renting out the facilities at the square to local people for funerals, weddings and other events. We have bookings virtually every weekend. The Elminians are happy to have such a good venue in town.

I must say that for the people here, the project is a life saver. Today tourism is clearly defined and structured in Elmina. Visitor inflow is peaking from virtually nothing to about 10–20 a day. Through this heritage project, Elmina now has a website; www.encounterelmina.com. I am updating our brochures and leaflets and a new marketing strategy will be out soon. More exciting times lie ahead for tourism in Elmina.

17 Back to basics

Name   : J. M. Yawson
Occupation : Contractor
Age   : 49 years
Children   : Five

Reconstructing our heritage – an opportunity

I am a permanent resident in Elmina. It is a small, quiet town. Construction work is virtually non-existent. So when I heard about the heritage project and the request to construction companies to put in bids for projects, I jumped at the opportunity, put in a bid and won the contract to renovate the four recreational centres for the Asafo companies, our local military groups.

These buildings are very special, the Asafo companies are important in our cultural tradition. When we started work on the buildings it was like the whole community was watching over our shoulders. The facades of the Asafo posts are decorated with statues, the once bright colours were faded and some had collapsed. When we took the statues in for reparation works, some people thought they had been stolen.

Original designs and techniques

The Project Management Unit did some research into the architectural designs. They were given to us to work with. The designs were captured based on the original plans of the buildings. This was done so that the old plan would be maintained. The roofing had to be redone, the concrete structures were all weak with age and indeed the statues needed some work on them. It was interesting to use the original construction techniques and train the workers to work with them. We want the youth to appreciate the value of our built heritage instead of the usual glass and concrete structures.

I recruited about 36 local people to support the construction activities. Contractors on the other projects did the same. I estimate that all in all over 150 jobs were created locally because of this project. The rehabilitation and renovation projects have improved the Elmina economy significantly. Elmina is lucky to have this support.

> When I heard the request to construction companies to put in bids for projects, I jumped at the opportunity, put in a bid and won the contract.

18 Culture & commitment

Name   : Mr D H Mensah
Occupation : Chairman Home Owners Association/District Education Officer
Age   : 64 years
Children   : Five

Elmina – a living museum
Elmina can best be described as a living museum. For 523 years Elmina encountered Europeans who left a lot of historical assets, mainly buildings of remarkable architecture. There used to be as many as 1200 such buildings but many have fallen into ruin, leaving less than 300 standing but in poor shape.

When the idea came up to boost tourism for Elmina through the heritage project, I and over one hundred owners of such historic buildings were invited to a meeting and informed about the plan to restore the old buildings. The buildings are to be attraction sites for tourists that will eventually lead to a boost in tourism for Elmina and generate income for the local people. Subsequently, our houses were inspected to ascertain their respective historical values.

Committing to the project
There was one condition for the renovation: part of the house was to be used to generate some income that could be ploughed back for maintenance. Additionally, we were told to ensure that the new use of the house would have to be of benefit to the whole community. We now have a bank, a pharmacy shop, a clinic, two guest houses and some new retail stores.

We were asked to form an association, which we did. As a sign of commitment, we were to pay 10 per cent of the cost of renovation before and after the completion, respectively. The monies were deposited in an account to be managed by the newly formed Home Owners Association.

Only 15 houses were restored but it has been worth it. The town looks livelier and tidier. In fact it has stimulated others who have not been able to take part in the scheme to also invest in the renovation of their houses. You can see building activity all over town. There is no doubt that this project has been very useful. The small amount done has had a major impact on the town and the promotion of Elmina as a tourist attraction site. It is important to take the project forward.

> The town looks livelier and tidier. In fact the project has stimulated others who have not been able to take part in the scheme to also invest in the renovation of their houses.

19 Location of choice

Name : Lankesha Ponnamperuma
Occupation : Group General Manager, Coconut Grove Hotels
Age : 36

Local footprint

Coconut Grove is a destination in itself. The beach resort takes advantage of the stunning coastline near Elmina and is the location of choice for many of the tourists that visit the Castle. The resort comprises private bungalows in a tropical garden setting, all with direct access to a secluded beach. Our conference facilities are the largest outside of Accra and attract a growing stream of business from the domestic market. We started in 1994 with 15 rooms and have since expanded to 50 rooms.

We also operate Bridge House, a bed & breakfast facility located directly opposite the Castle. It was the first merchant house built by the Dutch. As many of the other historic properties in town, the building was run down. In 2000 we took the initiative to restore the house and put it to commercial use. The B&B provides a unique opportunity for the guests to experience Elmina while residing in comfort in a historic building and to observe the everyday life of the inhabitants.

The company is wholly Ghanaian owned. We leave a positive footprint locally: 90% of our supplies is bought from local producers and we provide about 150 direct jobs for the local community.

Sustaining the returns of the project

We were happy to make our contribution to the Elmina heritage project. We particularly appreciated the emphasis on the general cleanliness of the town. I was in Elmina before the project took off and there were so many flies that all the insecticides in town put together would not have been able to clear them. Between 2000 and 2005 the basic medical bill for my staff was 15 million cedis annually. When the sanitation situation was tackled under the heritage project, the figure dropped to 2 million cedis.

Our clients maintain that *'there's always something new when you visit this paradise'*. They are duly impressed by the new look of the town. The situation has greatly improved and tourists who would normally not venture into town now do so. I can tell you that among all the destination sites in Ghana, Elmina is the only place that has seen development in infrastructure, largely due to the heritage project.

> I can tell you that among all the destinations sites in Ghana, Elmina is the only place that has seen development in infrastructure, largely due to the heritage project.

Team & Players:

Lead Agencies

Komenda Edina Eguafo Abrem (KEEA) District Assembly
Being the local administrative authority, the KEEA District Assembly spearheaded the project. They were the responsible entity for the development and implementation of the Elmina 2015 Strategy.

Urban Solutions
Urban Solutions, a Netherlands-based consultancy firm specialised in urban regeneration, was the key counterpart of the KEEA District Assembly throughout the process. Urban Solutions assisted the KEEA District Assembly in the formulation of the 2015 Strategy and acted as coordinating unit for the implementation of the 10 projects under the Elmina Heritage Project.

Ghana Museum and Monuments Board
As principal caretaker of all monuments in Ghana, GMMB has been involved in the project from the early stages. The Monuments Board played an important advisory role and they were also acting project supervisor for all restoration works affecting listed monuments.

National Authorising Officer (NAO)
The Ministry of Finance and Economic Planning was involved in the process in its function as National Authorising Officer for the European Development Fund.

European Commission Delegation in Ghana
The ECD in Ghana was involved in the process as one of the main funding agencies of the Elmina 2015 Strategy projects.

Collaborating Parties

Edina Traditional Council
The Edina Traditional Council is Elmina's traditional authority and cornerstone of Elmina culture. The council was an important communication channel between the PMU and the local community. Their participation in the project Steering Committee was essential for the success of the project and will continue to be crucial to embed future tourism related activities among the people of Elmina.
Ghana Heritage Conservation Trust and Ghana Tourist Board
Being the prime organisations in the country when it comes to heritage conservation and tourism development, GHCT and GTB were represented in the project Steering Committee as well as in a number of project working groups.

Government of Ghana
To make sure the project was fully embedded in the local jurisdiction, the project Steering Committee also had representatives of the Ghana National Commission on Culture and the Ministry of Local Government, Rural Development and Environment.

UNESCO
Finally, as the principal international player when it comes to safeguarding heritage, UNESCO was also a member of the project Steering Committee.

Consultants
Aid to Artisans Ghana (ATAG)
SNV, Organisation for International Development
OBAP Business Services
Strattcom Africa
Fritz Baffour
K.N.U.S.T. consultants
GW Consult
Tony Asare
Alex Awuku
QS Pro
Ablin Consult

Contractors
Memphis Construction Ltd.
Kendricks Construction Ltd.
De-bearach Ltd.
Davies Wright Ltd.
Sammy Ray Construction Ltd.
Sambethy Investment Ltd.
Llimpey Decon Ltd.
BCG Contract Works
Witlas Enterprises Ltd.
Allor & Sons Ltd.
Akaidoo Enterprises Ltd.

With Special Thanks to:
The Regional Minister, Central Region, Hon. Nana Ato Arthur; The former Minister for Tourism and Diasporan Relations, Hon. J. Obetsebi-Lamptey; The Senior Minister, Hon. J.H. Mensah; The National Authorising Officer for the EDF and the staff of the European Commission Delegation in Ghana, Janet Appiah, Vincent Ringenberg, Edouard van Vlasselaer, Dörthe Wacker and Huub and Abel.

The Elmina Heritage Project was realised with financial support from the European Commission, Dutch Culture Fund and the Royal Netherlands Embassy, Ghana.

Project Management Unit
Paul Schuttenbelt : Team Leader (1999–2005)
Dick ter Steege : Team Leader (2006–2007)
Ohene Sarfoh : Deputy Team Leader (2004–2005)
Josephine Akoto-Bamfo : Deputy Team Leader (2006–2007)
Anthony Annan-Prah : Local Project Coordinator
Nana Ekua Viala : Office Manager
Eric Sappor Accountant
Ester van Steekelenburg : Local Economic Development Expert
Cor Dijkgraaf : Housing Expert

Logistical support : Kakra, Emmanuel and Mavis

Special thanks to : Michel Doortmont (RUG), Peter van Dun, Jean-Paul Corten (RDMZ), Henri van der Zee, IHS – Rotterdam and ILGS – Accra.